THE REAL US
(and we're not crazy)

Dotty "Thea" Williams-Scalco

ACKNOWLEDGEMENTS

Gratitude: a feeling so overwhelming you can't sit still.

In 1985, I was a junior in college. I remember one afternoon sitting on a beach on Long Island, with my sister in law. I had recently changed my major from psychology to journalism. I was always fascinated with people and human behavior however I felt many approaches in the field of psychology didn't address the true spirit of the human.

My sister-in-law asked me what my plan was in the field of journalism.
I said, "I am going to write a book."
She asked, "About what?"
My response, "I don't know yet."

I dropped out of college, got married, raised 3 children and 23 years later, I now know!

It was my intuition, my deeper inner "knowing". Maybe it was my soul's agreement to come to this planet and help others by writing. Although my conscious wasn't aware of this, my spirit was.

About 6 months ago, in meditation, the inspiration for *The Real Us* came to me like a flash. This is how our guides, angels and the Alpha Omega work. They gently push, guide and support us and if we don't listen, then they ZAP YA.

I am grateful for the powers that be.

I am grateful for the many friends who have contributed to the making of The Real Us.

I am blessed to have Earth Angels in my life that literally saved me from the 'really bad days'.

Thank you, Linda Hack for finding me. Thank you, Joann Xydias for your dedication. Thank you, Angela Pavon, for your wisdom.

Thank you for all those who shared their stories:
>Denise Ramon
>John Railton
>John Fessel
>Sarah and Ian Horridge
>Joann Xydias
>Linda Lee Hack
>Michael Christopher
>James Newman
>Luna Trinity Ruby
>Carmen Marin
>Jennifer Holbrook
>Tom Zaimes
>Chris Johansen

I am truly blessed, with a multitude of people, places and things that have demonstrated to me, that we are bigger than our bodies. With our extrasensory abilities, we are a powerful source connected to All That Is.

I encourage everyone to keep exploring, there is so much to learn and experience. This thing called "life" truly is magical, even with all its twists, turns, bumps and bruises. And finally I want to thank a man I never met, but his channeled words helped me realize, *"Who I am, what I am, and how I serve"*

Thank you, Paul Selig, a humbling example of The Real Us.

Table of Contents

1. Am I Crazy?...................................'..........................9
2. Born Pure...13
3. Our Clairs...17
4. The Doorway to Higher Consciousness 23
5. Childhood Innocence...................................31
6. A Universal Language....................................37
7. Everything is Energy....................................43
8. Lost and Stolen Secrets...................................51
9. Reopening Our Toys in the Attic 63
10. Beyond the Veil.......................................71
11. Flying High...75
12. Light Beings.......................................83
13. Sleep, Perchance to Dream 89
14. Everyday People.....................................101

Introduction

Humans want to be touched by an angel, hear whispered words of divine wisdom and feel bounties of unconditional love. We see it in the movies, watch it on TV and read books about the miracles, but we doubt it can happen to us. Why have we bought into this belief?

What if, in the still of the night or the dawn of a new day, when all was quiet, you heard voices? What if touching people sent tingles up your arms and you could feel other people's pain? What if, in your time of loneliness, you saw an image that told you all was well?

What do you do? Who do you tell? Would others understand or would they call you crazy?

Being loved and accepted by others is so important to us. In fact, studies show that social acceptance is one of the top 8 basic desires of humans. It dates back to our tribal ancestors. No one wanted to be ousted from the clan for it meant facing the monsters of the forest or the barrens of the land all alone. Being part of a tribe meant safety.

If you stay inside the boundaries of your tribe and blend in nicely, you will be safe, but, go outside of those lines and chances are that you may get killed. You don't have to go far into the depth of the Congo to see this, just look at the gangs of our inner cities.

Today, as societies grow, we organize into cities, countries, religions and political parties, seeking shelter under the dogma of Mother Culture.

Although communities create a sense of being a part of something, they can also create separation.

Rules, requirements and prejudices tell us if we are bad, wrong, sick or different.

We are separated from those who are good, right, normal and healthy.

The bad go to jail, the sick go to a hospital, the old go to a home.. The weird and "mentally ill" are pushed aside, sometimes left homeless or suicidal.

How did this happen?

If you ask most people, they will claim there is one God that created and loves us all, yet we put labels on everyone we meet. What would happen if instead, we truly embraced the idea of an Alpha and Omega, an all knowing power that we are all connected to?

Would we then start to see each other in a different light, realizing we are more than just our bodies and minds, but that we are spirits?

Would seeing, hearing and feeling energies deepen our connection to each other?

Would we experience more miracles?

If the illusion of death and the wisdom of eternal life was ours, we could live in less fear. We could embrace cooperation instead of competition. We could work together for the benefit of all. Truth is, it is all possible. We are equipped with extrasensory abilities that keep us in touch with the wisdom of Mother Earth and Father Sky. We are electro-magnetic in nature, wired to external force fields. We hold a source of light that can penetrate our brethren's heart. We are chemically orchestrated to reach higher states of awareness and health.

As we break out of our spiritual closets the soul becomes visible and we are finally our true, authentic selves.

These are the stories and teachings of people who let go of the fears and exposed who they really are. These are people just like YOU!

THE REAL US (and we're not crazy)

Chapter 1
Am I Crazy?

"Crazy" has been used to describe myself and the others who bravely participated in the making of this book. When I was younger, crazy was good. I liked to ski down mountains at high speeds. I jumped off bridges and cliffs into the cold crisp waters. I danced wildly on the lawns of concert arenas. Crazy meant fun, carefree and fearless, but, as I got older, crazy got crazier.

I will start with my first close encounter of the ghostly kind. It occurred around the age of 8 or 9 while on a weekend venture with my parents. At the time, we were visiting some friends of my parents who had recently moved to the mountains of Pennsylvania. This was my first time in such a setting. I was from a middle class community on Long Island where homes lined up in perfect order, but, now I was surrounded by mountains and forests. On the way to our destination, we drove along empty roads with tattered buildings. My dad explained to me, that the town was once a booming area, but due to changes in the industry, businesses had shut down and people had lost their jobs. I could smell gloom seeping from the walls of the once vibrant structures.

When we pulled up into the driveway, I wasn't thrilled. The huge house on the hill was not inviting. Houses on Long Island were all fairly new with fresh paint and promising gardens, but this home had been sitting in these mountains much longer than anything I had ever seen. It struck me odd because the outside was lush and vibrant. The thickness of the trees was exhilarating to me. I was used to seeing rectangular mowed lawns. I suppose I expected the home to look happy, like a cabin owned by the 7 dwarfs. When I entered the house, I was surrounded by the beauty of wooden walls, but they were so desperately seeking attention. The air inside was stale. All I kept thinking about was how beautiful the outside was. I wanted to go find singing rabbits and dancing deer. During dinner, I made the suggestion that we go for a walk, but our hosts thought it was a bad idea. They told us about a big grizzly bear that once visited their back door. If you knew my parents, you would know that they wouldn't have any of that. Born and raised in the city of New York, big grizzlies meant torn limbs and kidney eating monsters.

I on the other hand, imagined a more enchanting meeting and secretly hoped I would see the magnificent creature, before I left.

Later that evening, as the adults continued with their catching ups, I retreated to a large room with two beds. My parents were to have the larger one and I was to sleep in the smaller bed against the wall. I was happy to be sharing a room with my parents as the house was unfamiliar. Little girls like having their mommy and daddy nearby in new environments.

Sometime in the middle of the night I was awoken. I do not believe there was a reason, such as a noise, but I recall just slowly opening my eyes to see what surrounded me. I gazed to the left and on the edge of my parents' bed, sat an old woman. Although the clothing, hair and facial features were complex and detailed, there was no density to the figure before me. She was just quietly resting as if it was a long day of tiring work. Her hands rested in her lap. Her attire consisted of a loose fitting house dress and apron. Her hair was long and pulled back in a bun with the ends hanging loosely. She was plump, in a matronly way. Her posture was one of solemn thought. She must have become aware that I had woken as she slowly turned her head and looked at me.

That was when I realized she was real. It wasn't an illusion from a foggy eyed kid; this thing was moving and breathing. Now, maybe not in the same sense that you and I breathe, but let's just say she was alive in some form or fashion. I screamed. It startled my parents as they both left their dream state to enter into my world. I looked over at them and then back towards the older woman, but she was gone.

My parents consoled me, letting me know it wasn't real and I was just having a bad dream. I wasn't convinced, but I had no other source of references to seek. Their answer was absurd to me as I knew I was fully awake. I had plenty of time to observe her before I made the conscious decision that she was not of this world. We made eye contact. She felt my presence and acknowledged my awakening. She spoke to me with emotion. There were no clear words, but she undoubtedly expressed to me that she was sadly lost and had no ideas on what to do. She had accepted the fact that she was stuck here, but extremely unpleased. This was not an apparition of a woman who wanted to play tricks on her new house guests, but a soul that had misplaced all that she once knew.

For years, I tucked that story away. The well meaning adults in my life had taught me not to pay any attention to foolish illusions.

Fast forward nearly 40 years, lying in bed meditating, a thought occurred to me: *Why not put together a collaboration of these stories?* I am sure it will help those who read them to feel more comfortable in sharing their experiences.

As I mentioned earlier, when we are accepted into a tribe, we feel safe. The tribe will grow and more will gather.

I contacted some folks within my tribe as I knew they would be eager to help and for this I am thankful!

But, first let's talk a little about some metaphysical, philosophical and even biological concepts.

Chapter 2
Born Pure

We come into this world, knowing exactly who we are. Everything is a wonder and delight. We are children of the Alpha and Omega. We are blessed with a multitude of gifts — too many to list. If we are raised in a nurturing home, we feel a sense of connection... someone that loves us and oh, how good that feels.

Unfortunately, not everyone is born into an environment of support and unconditional love. A child of God can be abandoned, abused, neglected and shamed. It doesn't make sense even to the infant's psyche: "I must have done something wrong".

Even in a "good home", with parents of the best intentions, feelings of abandonment and low esteem can occur when we are punished or told we were "bad".

This isn't bad parenting, it simply is a culture of attempting to raise kind kids who will, hopefully, obey the rules of society and be successful.

Since the days in the playground and sandbox, you have been conditioned to live in fear. Fear of not being accepted, wanted or good enough. But, how can that possibly be? It makes no sense to us because our spirit remembers emerging from a place of unconditional love. You may recall talking to angels or child-like spirits, but someone told you that was just your imagination. You may have even said your nightly prayers, but unless those practices and words were supported throughout your day, they eventually slipped from your mind.

As we grow older, we learn the ways of the world and forget the ways of the Kingdom. We become separated through our feelings of guilt. In many religions we are told that we were born into "sin" and you must be cleansed or "saved". Man, what kind of head trip is that? The only thing we need to be saved from is the indoctrination that we are not worthy.

It may take a lot of convincing for you to agree to that. It might take years for your consciousness to accept it, but every human being that is born comes with a knowing of their divine right. I believe one of the reasons we find our society so sad, is because we feel separate from the Holy. We have been denied our right to be who we truly are.

You are not here to claim your ticket stubs for each kind act you perform hoping to cash them in at the end of your journey. You are here to learn what your soul needs for its own growth and expansion. And guess what? What your soul needs is not the same thing your sister needs or what your co-worker or your son, or your neighbor needs to evolve. So telling others what to do and how to live based on your individual wants and needs, is not always the best advice. Each person has their own path with its own unique set of rocks, bumps and maybe even trenches. It is, however, the benefit of all when we lift our brothers and not scorn them for their trials.

Much like a baby who is learning to walk, you inspire and support them to get up and try again. With cheers and jeers you encourage them to take another step. You would never chastise or shame them because they had some stumbling moments.

You trust that they will get it eventually. And, why is this? Because we all know inside each baby is an innate, powerful source of potential. When and why did we stop trusting that for ourselves?

A wonderful addition to that is that we have come with the tools to help guide us. We are equipped with an internal GPS wired to a universal energy field of intelligence and love. It is this gift that enables us to create, relate, inspire and guide. It is our intuition... the inner technology that creates worlds!

THE REAL US (and we're not crazy)

Chapter 3
Our Clairs

Some say intuition is a mystical power, something of a spiritual talent only a few are capable of. Skeptics say it is a lucky guess, but, we all have it. Some on a level that is more advanced than others, but when we eliminate the fear and open up with acceptance our abilities expand.

Science is proving it as an intricate part of our multi-sensory perception. It helps us to KNOW beyond the norms of the intellect.

You can say, being intuitive is being in tune — in tune to your environment. We need this ability to survive. Our distant ancestors needed to know when and where there was danger. We were nomads, hunters and gatherers. We relied on Mother Earth for food, shelter and medicine. We had to know when it was safe to go outside our cave or dwelling. We had to 'sense' the tiger that was lurking or when a storm was brewing. These abilities went far and beyond our hearing and sight. By the time we saw the beast or storm cloud coming, it may have been too late. We had to rely on other sources. This source is our intuition and it works in many ways.

Most people are familiar with the "gut feeling". It has proven us right so many times. When you trust it, you are glad, when you don't you regret it. This is a clear signaling device to help you make an intelligent decision, one that was initially used to keep us alive. Now, we use it for business and buying decisions, relationship choices, and, yes, still for survival skills.

We hear stories of people saying, 'something told me not to get on that plane' as they learn about a devastating crash. Or, 'I got this weird feeling about that guy', when they discover he was recently arrested for a violent crime.

So, if it is a "knowing" why do we call it a "gut feeling"? Science is now showing our gut contains more neurons than our spinal cord and peripheral nervous system (network of nerves that line our spinal cord and brain).

Information is detected in our guts sometimes before our brain can digest it. Without diving deeper into biology, a simple idea for you to consider is that every cell is alive with tiny finger-like protrusions (cilium) on their walls. These act like sensors instructing the cell how to behave and adapt. There are 50 trillion of these babies, constantly communicating with every system in our body, giving and receiving information.

Now add the microbes that our gut contains and the numbers increase.

Remember, our innate drive is to survive. Each and every cell is equipped to assist.

We know our brain and gut talk when we are nervous, stressed or excited. Sure these are emotions that trigger a chemical re-action, but, all emotions begin with a thought. We think about getting the results from the lab test or going on a job interview and our nerves begin to make our stomach queasy. We anticipate seeing the guy or gal we really like and we get butterflies in our belly.

When we know something beyond reason we call it a "gut feeling" because when the brain is saying "yes" or "no", so is the gut.

In metaphysics, we call this "claircognizance". You can equate it to an automatic download on your computer or digital device. Instantly, you have a knowing and it comes as quickly as a push of the Enter key.

Another form of intuition is "clairsentience". This takes "feeling" to another level. This is when we get sensations in our own physical body that comes from an outside source.

When someone says, "I feel your pain", they are literally feeling the pain. This is actually one of my strongest Clairs, as they are called.

When I am in tune with someone, I can feel all sorts of things in my body. I can tell if they have any kind of pain, blockage or health problems. Strange thing is sometimes these 'aches' or issues were things that happened years ago.

Now, let's move on to some other Clairs. Most people have heard the term "clairvoyant". This is when a person "sees things". Now this is a big one because it can happen in so many ways. You can see things in your mind's eye, and we all do this when we day dream or visualize. But, the ability to see often occurs with our eyes closed.

During our sleeping hours, we dream. Some of our dreams are

just our mind trying to empty the day's thoughts and worries, but, much of it can be showing you a very important message. Many people talk about a solution to a problem occurring during a dream, musicians hear songs, artists see paintings.

But, even during the waking hours when our eyes are closed, we can have these visions. Eliminating outside stimuli and clearing the mind can bring on all sorts of symbols, lights, figures and scenarios. There are often moments in meditation that we have insight, clarity, visions of the future or an incredibly creative idea. In fact, the concept of this book came to me during mediation, but it didn't come as a vision. That brings us to the next Clair- "clairaudient".

Clairaudient is the ability to hear. This one is a bit hard to explain if you have never experienced it before. It doesn't always (and most often not) come as a voice outside or even inside your head. Although I have had this happen to me, (I share a story in chapter 5), it is more commonly a gentle whisper that speaks to your thoughts. I have had some people ask me, "how do you know it isn't just your thought or your own voice?" and all I can say, is "Oh, you will know". There is a distinct difference.

We all have that little voice in our heads that some may call the angel and devil that sit on our shoulders and whispers into our ears, but, that is just your conscious. Clauraudient is a clear message from something outside yourself and this is when you have no other choice but to BELIEVE (or to think you are crazy).

There is something outside of ourselves that is talking to us, watching us, guiding and guarding us. We are never alone, and they want to communicate. They have always been here, but now perhaps for the first time since the shutting of the veil as I will call it, they are contacting us at an increasing rate. No longer are the prophets, healers, mediums, channelers and alchemists being taunted as the weird few.

Our frequency as a planet and species is rising — it has to. We are back to survival mode as our oceans, forests, wildlife and humans are in turmoil. We are asking, seeking, praying for unity and peace. And, as we do this, we are expanding in thought, ideas, innovation and awareness. Universal Intelligence... The Alpha and the Omega... the angels and the guides know our thoughts, feel our wounds, see our suffering and hear our words. They are sending answers and the solution to our struggles is **US**. *We* are what the planet has been asking for... a new and evolved species that is in tune and communes with our inner and outer environment.

The intuitive, mystic, shaman and the everyday folk are all experiencing an awakening of the senses. Our bodies, minds and spirits are uniting with the non physical energies that unconditionally love and support us.

THE REAL US (and we're not crazy)

Chapter 4
The Doorway to Higher Consciousness

Located near the center of the brain is the pineal gland .It is a very small organ shaped like a pine cone (which is where it gets its name). It is reddish-gray in color and only about 1/3 inch long.

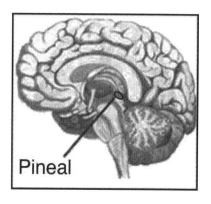

Pineal

The pineal gland regulates our sleep, hunger, thirst and sexual drives. So, as you can see, it is essential for survival. Today, most of us can go to our refrigerator if we are hungry and turn on a faucet if we are thirsty. You can even pick up the phone or go online if you are in need of a little "action". But, it wasn't always that way. As I stated in the previous chapter even before we began farming and domesticating animals, we had to hunt and gather.

It was hard enough to find food, never mind a mate. But, we survived, progressed and procreated. One of the reasons why is because of our inner GPS.

The brain's pineal gland contains magnetite. Magnetite is a crystal that literally acts as an antenna for external electromagnetic fields. It is what informs the whales, moose and other migratory mammals on their position as they travel. It interacts with external electromagnetic fields over a million times more strongly than any other biological substance. These magnetic frequencies are picked up as sound. One can say the whales can hear where they are and which direction they should go. (Perhaps we can call them clairaudient?). It helps migratory animals find their home, food and even a mate.

Many civilizations still rely on hunting. They have a very keen sense of nature's vibratory field. They are in touch with the animal and plant kingdom much more than advanced cultures. I use the term advanced loosely, because I believe it our disconnect with Mother Earth that is contributing to much of our illness and depression, but I will leave that topic for my next book in this series. We may not need a pineal gland to locate a herd of gazelle to hunt, but we can use our complex Global Positioning System to assist us in maneuvering through our lives.

What I find even more fascinating is the fact that the pineal gland produces a compound called Dimethyltryptamine (DMT). This natural narcotic is also found in plants, fungi and various animals. After 49 days of conception the pineal gland is visible in the developing fetus and the unborn child is already receiving DMT.

Dr. Rick Strassman, the leading researcher in the field of DMT, calls it the "spirit molecule."

"When our individual life force enters our fetal-body, the moment in which we become truly human, it passes through the pineal and triggers the first primordial flood of DMT."

Oddly enough, large amounts of DMT flood the brain at the time of birth and at the time of death. The 49 day mark for the pineal gland to develop in a fetus may hold some significance since the Tibetan Buddhists believe that is the amount of time it takes a soul to reincarnate into another body. Yep! Forty Nine days.

Science is also showing us that higher amounts of DMT are released during elevated spiritual occurrences as well as near-death experiences.

During one of Dr. Strassman's experiments he injected his volunteers with a plant-based DMT. His subjects reported a wide range of hallucinogenic experiences, including visiting other dimensions.

Some people with head injuries release extremely high levels of DMT and report experiences very similar to schizophrenia. Instead of the medical industry quickly prescribing drugs for those with schizophrenic episodes, perhaps they should be looking into DMT. Could a head injury be responsible for what physicians want to label as a "mental illness"?

We know heavy metals and man-made chemicals can cross the blood brain barrier.

Is our pineal gland being triggered to release elevated amounts of DMT due to an injury or toxin exposure?

DMT production occurs naturally in the body, but the indigenes natives of the Amazon have been ingesting DMT for thousands of years by brewing a tea from various plants.

They performed ceremonies using the concoction to contact and experience the "higher realms."

In many cultures, shamans actually consider "schizotypal personality disorder" a gift to the community. Those with the symptoms are supported by their family and peers and taught how to control their episodes. People with the ability to reach and communicate with other dimensions are considered very intelligent and beneficial. These people are nurtured, loved and highly respected. It all goes back to being a part of a tribe where you are safe and accepted. All members are considered important and play a role. What Western cultures do to "abnormal" people is truly a crime and a disservice to everyone.

During chemical experimentation in 1931, DMT was synthesized in a lab, but its psychedelic properties were unknown until 1956 when Hungarian chemist and psychiatrist, Stephen Szara read about certain plants used by the South American shamans. Oddly, Szara escaped Hungary, immigrated to the U.S and worked for the National Institute of Health for thirty years. Hmm?

DMT is considered the most potent psychedelic known to man and our brain produces it every day. My guess is Szara shared his knowledge. It is also my assumption that the secrets of plants are deliberately kept for pharmaceutical greed. Today, the proof of THC and CBD in cannabis to heal is overwhelming.

In the 1990s scientists officially discovered what they are calling the endocannabinoid system, named after cannabis plants. Apparently we have receptors sites in our cells that utilize cannabis. Just like DMT, our bodies naturally produce THC (and other compounds found in marijuana). These endocan.. noids are synthesized to create a state of balance within our immune system.

As medical marijuana explodes, big agriculture and pharma are doing their best to gain control over its access. I believe we are winning, however. There is a quintessential element to our plants and it too is a gift from an all knowing, all healing Creator. As Western cultures get privy to this information, we will see plant medicine exploding. It has already begun.

The French philosopher and mathematician Reneì Descartes was also fascinated with the pineal gland. He regarded it as the *"principal seat of the soul, and the place in which all our thoughts are formed."*

Although Decartes still had much to learn, what he discovered in the 1600's is pretty wild.

Descartes noticed then when people try to remember things, they tend to look up. When people think they look down. The diagram he drew shows the pineal gland's position as we look up and down.

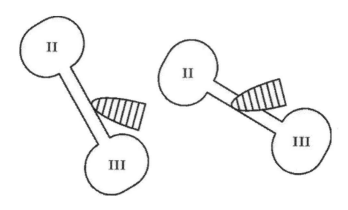

...oking up raises the gland and opens the passage, ...ior ventricle where he believed memories were ...e who want to think, on the other hand, look down beca...s lowers the gland, closes the passage, and protects the spirit in the middle ventricle from being disturbed by memories stored in the posterior. You don't need an anatomy or biology degree to see he might have been on to something.

This got me thinking about some of my earlier training. In Theta Healing, we are taught to focus on the pineal gland and imagine going UP (to the Creator of All That Is). This technique always worked for me and I still use it today, when I am seeking assistance from spirit.

It also got me thinking that "memories" aren't just stored in the brain, but floating in the ethers. Everything vibrates and holds a frequency. The human's eyes and ears can only see and hear frequencies up to a certain point. It doesn't mean the higher frequencies don't exist. We have sound waves, gamma rays, ultraviolet rays, etc. We know the brain also works in waves and frequencies. Is it possible that every word or thought expressed is still buzzing around the universe? When we look up or open up our "passage" is it then when our intuitive and psychic thoughts, images and messages come flooding in?

Because of its location in the brain and its connection to light, the pineal gland is also called the "third eye". The pineal organ contains photoreceptor cells much like the human eyes. Receiving light will trigger the gland to lower production of melatonin. Melatonin is the hormone that regulates the sleep cycle. Sleep is crucial for optimal health and sleep is where dreams occur. We will look more at dreams later on.

Not only does the gland contain neurons, which are cells that receive process and transmit information through electrical and chemical signals, but it also contains glial cells. The glial cells primary function is to protect the gland from other neurons and to clean up any dead neurons. This pineal gland must be very significant since it sits on top of our nervous system like antennae and is highly protected and regularly cleaned.

But, ancient religions and cultures didn't study glands, hormones and neurons, yet, we see images of pine cones and the third eye in just about every sacred practice.

You often see the pine cone shape on top of the heads of Buddha. The Assyrian deities are often shown holding a pine cone. Many gods are shown holding a staff with a pine cone proudly sitting on top (Osiris - Egyptian; Dionysus and Bacchus - Greek). Even the Catholic Pope's staff depicts a pine cone under the cross of Jesus. And, here is a doozy... the largest pine cone statue ever created by the Romans sits in front of the Vatican!

The Egyptian Eye of Horus was a symbol of protection, royal power and good health. It was used to personify the goddess Wadjet. A similar eye; the Eye of Ra was used as a symbol to represent goddesses such as Hathor, Sekhmet and others.

Fast forward and we notice that the *"all seeing eye"* is on the hand of Fatima (named after Muhammad's daughter). It is also part of the masonry symbol and of course atop the pyramid on the U.S. dollar bill.

In The Sermon on the Mount, Jesus says: *The light of the body is the eye: if therefore thine eye be single, thy whole body shall be full of light. But if thine eye be evil, thy whole body shall be full of darkness.* (Matt 6:22-23, KJV)

Could Jesus have been talking about the third eye, the pineal gland?

Edgar Cayce, *"the sleeping prophet,"* is considered one of the most revered psychics in America with over 14,000 documented readings. Letters from all over the world with questions and health concerns would be answered by Cayce while he was in a trance. Although he had no formal knowledge of natural remedies, he often prescribed them to his followers. Because of this, he was also deemed the father of holistic medicine. Cayce was a devout Christian who claimed he received the information from Source.

He was quoted as saying, *"Keep the pineal gland operating and you won't grow old. You will always be young."*

I think we have enough evidence here to sufficiently claim, we are equipped and wired to make contact! Just who is it we are reaching?

Chapter 5
Childhood Innocence

Being a mother of three, I must say little children are such a delight and wonder. I clearly can recall incidences when my children said or did things that one may declare as odd. However, these occurrences became so often, that I had no choice but to pay attention. I was fortunate to be able to homeschool all of them, so I did spend more time with them then the average American mom and I am so grateful that I did.

Being there for their first words is wonderful, but I was able to be there when my baby girl started speaking of things no "normal" 2 year old would speak of. She had facts and information that did not come from any source I exposed her to. She was the one who had me questioning the after-life and past lives. She was without a doubt a wise old soul. In fact, she once told me she was the second coming. When I remind her of this now, she laughs and says she was just kidding, but, I don't think so. I was there when she said it and there was no joking in her tone or face. Besides, I am not even sure how she knew about the concept of a savior returning. It certainly was not discussed in our home.

For years, that moment in time flashes back to me. I often wondered what exactly did she mean and where did that come from? I knew she was serious, I also knew she was an extension of pure God/Source that spoke through her innocence.

One may assume the second coming is the return of a Christ, but what I recently learned is the concept of volunteers coming to Earth to help us out, to move us along more quickly. Perhaps what she meant was that she was part of the second wave of volunteers.

Dolores Cannon, a hypnotist, was seeing a thread with thousands of her clients. In a trance, many of her clients talked about the beauty of the afterlife and that they did not want to return. However, the Earth was in trouble, so they decided to come back as volunteers to assist in raising the frequency of the planet and its inhabitants.

After categorizing her subjects by their current age, she noticed three (3) distinct generations of souls. What I read so far seems to be pretty darn accurate. I myself fit in the first category: a generation of souls who often go against the status quo, horrified by violence and deeply disturbed over emotions of anger and hate. This generation is prone to suicide because they just cannot emotionally handle the state of chaos the Earth is currently in.

The second generations of souls are the volunteers and they are in their 20s, 30s and early 40s. They tend to work quietly on their own, effecting people in a positive way behind the scenes. Just their presence brings much needed love and light. Ironically, they are here to share their energies, but do not really like being around people. That's my girl!

For further reading about all three generations, you may want to check out, The Three Waves of Volunteers and the New Earth, by Dolores Cannon.

This next story is from John Fessel's childhood. On our first meeting, I felt something really strong emanating from John. He is in the age group of the second wave and I can see in his spirit that he is a true seeker with the intentions to help others. He speaks about energy healing a bit later in the book, but for now, here is another sweet story of being a child.

I have been I around paranormal type activity my entire life. The first I realized something was different was when I was younger. I was about ten years old. I can remember walking out of my bedroom, through the living room and into the kitchen. My mom was in the kitchen making lunch. I walked through the living room and saw my mom had invited a friend over.

She was an older lady with short bright white hair, glasses, and very petite. She was wearing a navy-blue dress with sunflowers all over it. When I returned to the kitchen, I asked my mom who the lady was on the couch. My mom said there was no one on the couch! She claimed it was my imagination so I forgot about it.

A few years later when I was at the home of my grandmother, we were sitting around going through old photos. I saw a picture of that same lady wearing that same dress! I immediately asked who it was. It turns out she was a relative who had passed away before I was born. Her name was Alice. When Alice died my dad purchased her home and that was where we were living.
John Fessel, Florida Reiki Practitioner

Are you talking to me?

We may have all seen a "ghost" as a kid or heard of someone who has. Silly childish ghost stories aren't rare. We laugh, thinking how cute, then dismiss them. But, as I got older they began to talk to me... the first time it happened was a bit freaky. I was at a friend's house watching television. I will call him "Shawn", although that is not his real name.

I was lying on the couch and Shawn was seated right next to me on the floor. I guess you can say he was my boyfriend or whatever that means at 14. His parents' were not home. In fact, no one was there except us. Besides the sounds coming from the TV, the huge house was very quiet. When I reflect on that afternoon, I can still see both of us very vividly. There was a sense of nervousness on his part and I wasn't feeling fully comfortable myself. Perhaps I was feeling his unease. While trying to settle in and enjoy the program I suddenly heard the words: *"Get out!"*

I looked over at Shawn who was still glaring at the television.

"What?" I asked quite confused.

He looked at me puzzled.

"What did you just say?" I asked again.

"I didn't say anything," he promised.

I figured I must have imagined it, and went back to watching the show. Then I heard it again, but this time it was much louder: *"GET OUT!"*.

I knew at that point it wasn't Shawn, because the voice was one of a grown man; very strong and insistent.

"Did you hear that?"

"What? No, I didn't hear anything."

I told him what I heard twice. He reassured me, that it wasn't him, but he appeared a little spooked. I had the sense he believed me, but didn't want to talk about it and instead he suggested that we leave.

Shawn and I didn't stay together for long, but we remained friends. For a long time I found it odd that he never again asked me to come over. He lived on the next block and sometimes I would stop by, but I was never invited in.

Many years later, about the age of 18 or so, Shawn shared some personal stories with me. It turned out his home was one of extreme violence and abuse. It was heart breaking to hear. It all made sense now. When you come from that environment, you don't want friends over. I have no doubt that there has been a dark force in that home that didn't approve of my presence. I suppose he was doing me a favor.

THE REAL US (and we're not crazy)

Chapter 6
A Universal Language

When you experience paranormal activity as a very young child, you assume everyone else does as well. It just seems normal to you. It is not until you start talking about it to others that you realize these visions, verbal messages and sensations are not infused into every day conversation. This is where the idea of being crazy begins to fester in your mind. During my initiation into the extraordinary, I didn't think I was crazy, but, as life progressed, the experiences became stranger and stranger. I shared my stories with those I felt comfortable with. The reactions were not always what I expected and I could sense some of those closest to me were a bit freaked out by my tales. Thankfully, they were kind enough not to tell me to my face that I was nuts, but I can sense what they were thinking. With grace and kindness they would just smile and silently wish I got back on my rocker. I so enjoyed my supernatural experiences, but really wished I had someone to share them with... ...then I met Linda.

A little background as to why I was at the local health food store where Linda and I found each other: in the year 2000, my second child was labeled autistic. I knew he was not born with the symptoms he was expressing and one night, next to my son's bed, I prayed for answers. On my knees, I made a vow that if God gave me solutions, I would never stop teaching others. Many of those answers came to me from inspiration, intuition and divine synchronicities. I discovered alternative healing and energy medicine and to this day, I find ways to share what I have learned. On this particular day, I was at Nutrition S'mart giving a class on the heart chakra. The crowds are often small in this town, but they are never dull.

It is a given that after my talks someone from the audience will approach me with personal questions or insights. This day was no different. The woman in the front row had lots to ask. She stayed by my side as I packed up my laptop. Eager to go home, I was not giving our chat a whole lot of effort until she said something I had never heard before and then she had my full attention.

"I would like to stay in touch with you and talk more."

"Sure, that sounds great, I responded with my mind focused on the exit. You have my card, give me a call."

"I speak Light Language."

I stopped in my tracks, glared over at her and said, "WHAT?" with a profound desire to hear more.

Light Language has also been called speaking in tongues. I was familiar with the concept. I had seen some people performing this act at an evangelistic church I had attended with "Shawn" (remember him?), but my idea of someone speaking tongues was when an individual experienced the overpowering presence of the Holy Spirit. I figured Jesus spoke a foreign language, so why wouldn't they? I wasn't really surprised or impressed when I first experienced it, I figured anything was possible. Who am I to say it isn't real. But, outside of that church, I never heard it spoken again, nor had anyone even mentioned it. I blew it off as being one of those things at that weird church.

When I finally got the chance to hear Linda speak, I was mesmerized. The sounds were speaking to my soul, although my mind didn't understand the words. I intuitively knew that my higher self understood the message — I am sure you are familiar with the expression, "it moved me." Well, Light Language physically vibrates with your being. I now know why the monks chant or why the Tibetans use singing bowls. Something inside is shifting!

Research is now showing us that music and tones affect us both emotionally and physically. The higher the octave, the more we benefit. Dopamine, the "feel-good hormone", is released when we listen to songs we like. Prolactin, a bonding hormone, is released when you listen to music with another person; and, get this, if you sing with the other person, oxytocin is released, which creates a feeling of trust. Oh, boy, does that explain a lot?

Light Language is not just an overzealous utterance from an unsuspecting soul, Light Language is a gift channeled to those who are open to receive it.

Linda speaks:
As a young girl, my older sister and I would spend a few weeks with our great grandmother and her husband in Los Angeles where they lived. They were both Pentecostal pastors at Amy McPherson Four Square Church. This was my first real exposure to formal religious services. We went on Wednesday nights to what was called The 500 Room. That is where grandpa would preach. On Sundays, we went into the main church. It was very large with two or three stories. I had never seen a room that big being that I was from rural San Diego. The rooms above the main floor of church included museum-like displays of pictures

and medical equipment of those who had been healed. As a child, I found this to be an amazing place. It had back staircases that led to rooms we could not go in and metal staircases outside like a fire escape. My sister and I would play hide and seek there. As a child these were impressive times for me.

When I was about 12, I was sent by myself to care for my great grandmother who had fallen and broken both of her wrists. My great grandfather also needed help with his meals and bathing.

Looking back, it was a lot of responsibility for 12 year old child. It was during that stay, that I was spiritually over taken with the calling to come forward and give my heart to God. That is when I was filled with the Holy Spirit and given this gift of what at that time was called "speaking in tongue." The urge would come over me to speak in this tongue, and my great grandmother schooled me on how to use it, but, only in church. I had no idea what I was saying when I spoke in this unknown language, but, there was always someone in the congregation that would interpret what I was saying.

When I returned home, this gift I had received was put on hold as I did not have anyone there to nurture it. It was only during these past few years that I came across the words and concept of "Light Language" and started investigating it and its purpose.

At this time, I feel that my Light Language comes from LOVE and enters into the soul of the person to whom it is directed and inspires the release of Love within that person. Love can never hurt. Love is not to be feared. It can be healing and will be the foundation of the New Earth.

Linda Lee Hack, Florida
www.ChannelingByLindalee.com

Linda and I have been friends ever since that afternoon. I must say, I am so proud of her! Like all of us in this book, we had skills, beyond the five senses of human density that we kept secret in the unseen corners of our souls.

For over 40 years, Linda's gifts sat dormant. Thanks to the Internet, Linda was very fortunate to find information and connect to the people that would assist her in opening up her gifts. She began giving sessions through Skype, but most of her clients were from far away. People she never met. This was a giant leap for her, but, it is easy to hide behind a keyboard or a computer monitor. We do sessions with the lights out, so to speak. Behind closed doors we become vehicles and transmitters of spiritual communications. But, when the morning comes and it is time for us to face the norms of our culture, we hide our light. Inside of us, we each hold a fear; the fear of what will happen if we are discovered. Will we be crucified or burned at the stake like those in the past. Telling friends and family is one thing, because we know many of those close to us will still love us no matter how whacked out we appear, but, what about the public? Will we be called witches and warlocks and verbally stoned? Although, the western cultures seem to becoming more and more open minded, I have been called a fraud and a liar. I have even been told that my beliefs in the chakras, (energy centers) and meditation practices are evil. Yes, even yoga is of the devil. Jesus is the way, the only way to God and anything outside of him is the Anti Christ.

This is all based on fear. No one featured in this book has a fear of being eternally burned in a fiery hell, because we have learned to trust our own hearts. When you come to this planet in service, you are supported. It took a long time for many of us to realize this because of our strong desire to be accepted by our peers.

Later on, I will discuss fear and how eliminating it can bring us all closer, not only with each other, but with the universal Creator of All That IS!

Chapter 7
Everything is Energy

What exactly is energy medicine? You may already know much about the subject or you may know very little, but, let's talk about it anyway. In simple terms, everything is energy. Thought and words are even energy but we often equate movement with energy. "That kid's got a lot of energy," we may say while observing him do back flips off the sofa. It would be safe to say a sleeping dog has little energy. But, whatever the level of energy is, all matter contains vibrating molecules, atoms, sub atoms and quantum particles. Science keeps digging deeper and deeper into the body and mind, but, the more they search, the more they are coming out of the spiritual closet themselves. Many are finally confessing something exists far more powerful than the strongest microscope can capture and they are calling it GOD.

A few guys, who are making a huge impact on combining neuroscience and spirituality, are Dr. Joe Dispenza, Dr. Bruce Lipton and, my favorite, Gregg Braden. I highly suggest their work.

There are various terms for the energy that flows within us: life force, spirit, essence. This energy runs through our organs, bones, tissues, cells and so on. When this life force gets stuck, it can cause dis-ease or dis-comfort. Any major organ that has stagnated energy simply will not function at optimal levels. A failed organ will lead to serious ailments. In essence, we need to flow. My mom used to say *"the trick to a long life is to stay active, because you never saw a moving corpse."* We need to move externally and internally.

Energy medicine or healing is anything that assists in getting things moving. It could be massage, acupuncture and chiropractic. It could be foods or herbs that have anti- inflammatory properties. Many essential oils work in the same medicinal manner and would definitely be considered energy therapy. We are now seeing an upsurge in these plant medicines; as well as, CBD oils from hemp. When something works, it works. Homeopathy is one of my favorite forms of energy medicine and it has been showing incredible results. Although main stream medicine would prefer you didn't know about these methods, any quick search from reputable sources will show Westerners are clearly missing out on a key component to optimal health — all without serious side effects, no less.

This concept of moving energy is not new. This concept has been around for thousands of years — Prana, chi and vital force are just some of the other names used to describe this life energy. Acupuncture and Ayurveda are both Eastern forms of healing based on our life force and moving chi that date back over 5,000 years. Cave drawings in Egypt, show a man rubbing another's foot. Could this be a depiction of what we now call reflexology — a form of massage that works on meridian points? And, the most popular of all, is hands on healing performed by Jesus.

Energy medicine fascinates me and I now teach a form of energy medicine called Integrated Energy Therapy. Stevan J. Thayer, once an engineer, claimed to be visited by Archangel Ariel. Through him, she channeled a form of healing based on the idea that we hold emotions in our organs and cells. Steven had no prior knowledge of this concept and he wasn't very "religious".

Now, talk about feeling crazy... ...how do you think he felt when he left his job to become an ordained minister and opened The Center of Being? It took a lot of courage, but once you are called, you have to go.

As our energetic fields open, we are often led down the path to seek further expansion. With over 55,000 students now, Integrated Energy Therapy is growing and I am proud to be one of the 275 Master Instructors who teach globally. Being introduced to this form of energy healing was very profound for me. It truly opened up my intuitive abilities. But, I have to admit, like others in this book, I was a bit scared to let this information out. Let's face it, when you tell someone they have anger towards their dad stuck in their liver, they might think you are cuckoo. But, what is fascinating about I.E.T. is that its philosophies are very much in alignment with Eastern schools. Sure, maybe acupuncturists don't use the power of the angelic realm (knowingly), but something is assisting them in using their intuition to find blockages

I remember many years ago, I was taking my son to see a naturopath in Ft. Lauderdale. We were seeing great progress with Dr. Snyder and learning so much. During one visit, while touching my son, he closed his eyes and became silent. When he opened his eyes, he said something about my son's condition that has slipped my mind because I was more interested in his procedure. I asked him, "What did you just do?"

He said, "I asked the body what it needed."

Yes, it sounded odd, but I trusted him. Dr. Snyder is deserves all the credit for introducing me to new ways to look at health and illness.

Here is more from John Fessel:

When I was about 16, I started getting into energy work. I didn't even know what "energy work" was. I just had a friend who was very sick. She was not getting any help from doctors. I felt guilty. I was healthy and strong. No pain. I would watch her cry in the fetal position, just overwhelmed and in shock because of pain. So, through love I would just place my hands on her and ask "God" (I was a little more religious back then), to take some of my health and give it to her and let me take some of her pain. Well, it worked! I would sit for an hour or two. With my hands touching her skin and I would just start sweating from the heat exchange. I could not heal her. But, I gave her a couple hours of relief! Which was life changing! She could fall asleep! Like I said, I didn't heal her and she did finally find a doctor that helped her and she is fine now. But, ever since I gave her some relief, she told one of her friends. That friend had a botched knee surgery. She would come over and I would do the same thing. I didn't know this girl so I would just imagine that she was my friend and push my healthy energy into her knee and pull the pain out. Well, as awkward as it might have been, it helped. After coming to see me she began taking a quarter of the pain medicine she would normally need to function! That was huge!

(Note: Reducing her medication was her decision and not John's suggestion. An unlicensed energy healer cannot diagnose and treat. Well actually they have the ability to, but law says they cannot. If everyone went around healing each other the pharmaceutical industry would have a lot to lose.)

She had a boyfriend and all he knew was that she was coming over to some guy's house and that guy was touching his girlfriend. I invited him over to see what we were doing. He got upset and said, "Dude, who do you think you are, Jesus Christ or something?" I was upset. That was the last thing I wanted anyone to think about me. So, I stopped doing energy work for a long time. Years went by and I didn't practice because of that little comment. It wasn't until I heard about Reiki that I got back into it. Even at first I was standoffish. But, now energy work is important part of my life and I recommend everyone try it out.

Reiki is a form of energy healing that originated in Japan. The word Reiki is made of two Japanese words - Rei which means God's Wisdom and Ki which is life force energy. So Reiki is actually "spiritually guided life force energy."

We know hands-on healing is not new. The early followers of Jesus' teachings were made up of several groups. One such group was the Gnostics. They practiced the laying on of hands and professed to have a secret knowledge that was passed on to them by Jesus and His disciples. Their core beliefs were that the Kingdom of Heaven is within, and they relied on inspiration and inner guidance.

In 1938, Reiki reached the United States and is now becoming quite popular. You can find Reiki circles forming in churches, hospitals, yoga studios and metaphysical stores. Reiki uses the concept of a Universal life force that does the healing. Much like the life force within you, there is also a force above, below and around you. Reiki practitioners connect to this life force and through their hands they transfer it to you. This can have tremendous benefits.

Reiki is gaining popularity because people are feeling results. But, you don't have to be a practitioner to know the power of touch. The easiest way to experience energy healing is simply through touch. We all know how great a sincere hug feels or the sensation of someone combing their fingers through our hair.

When it is done with love, you are receiving healing. The best part is the person doing the touching receives healing as well. Studies show petting an animal is very therapeutic. Animal therapy is used in retirement homes, special needs facilities and more.

I continually hear stories from people who say that their hands begin to vibrate or heat up when they touch others. Although you do not need years of classes or certification to heal others with your hands, some chose to do so to better understand and enhance their abilities. Just like anything else; with proper training one can apply their skills more effectively.

She's got the power

A dear friend of mine who wishes to remain anonymous says she has been doing hands on healing for years.

"It's my own little secret," she says. "When a loved one is suffering, I can easily find the issue. My hands begin to tingle intensely when I find the spot," she says. "With touch and focus, within minutes, the pain and tension is gone."

"Why don't you want me to mention your name?" I asked her.

"It is not because I am scared," she said. "I just like knowing that it is my special gift from the Holy Spirit. It is one of the nine."

"What?"

"Yes, the nine gifts from the Holy Spirit. We all have them. My gift is healing."

"I never heard of that", I said.

"It's in the Bible," she said. "I don't remember them all, but one of them is the power to heal others."

"Get the heck out of here," I said. "You mean to tell me it is written in scripture?"

"Yes, look it up"

So I took out my handy dandy smart phone and searched. I couldn't believe my eyes.

There it in was Corinthians 12 KJV:
[1] Now concerning spiritual gifts, brethren, I would not have you ignorant. [2] Ye know that ye were Gentiles, carried away unto these dumb idols, even as ye were led. [3] Wherefore I give you to understand, that no man speaking by the Spirit of God calleth Jesus accursed: and that no man can say that Jesus is the Lord, but by the Holy Ghost. [4] Now there are diversities of gifts, but the same Spirit. [5] And there are differences of administrations, but the same Lord. [6] And there are diversities of operations, but it is the same God which worketh all in all. [7] But the manifestation of the Spirit is given to every man to profit withal. [8] For to one is given by the Spirit the word of wisdom; to another the word of knowledge by the same Spirit; [9] To another faith by the same Spirit; to another the gifts of healing by the same Spirit; [10] To another the working of miracles; to another prophecy; to another discerning of spirits; to other diverse kinds of tongues; to another the interpretation of tongues: [11] But all these worketh that one and the selfsame Spirit, dividing to every man severally as he will.

"It says it right here as clear as day, right in the Corinthians."

"Yes," she said.

"So, how come so many Christians think all this stuff is evil?" I asked.

"Because most people don't read the Bible; they throw Scripture around, but don't really study it."

As I look at these gifts and I reflect on all the stories my friends have shared, I want to cry. We aren't crazy. Not one bit. Instead, WE ARE BLESSED.

Chapter 8
Lost and Stolen Secrets

Why would being called "Jesus" or something be so frightful for John?

Remember, research shows being accepted is #8 on our list of human needs.

Being different is kind of cool, but being a freak sucks.

What could possibly happen if we displayed our divine gifts?

If we use Jesus as an example, it is pretty easy to see — we will be crucified.

Using our innate powers is seen as a "no-no" and for many reasons. Using the crucifixion of Jesus was a clear message, threaten the throne of the emperor and you will be killed. Jesus wasn't trying to take the throne, but He was gaining a following. People were listening. He was teaching them about the Holy Ghost and the powers each of us has within.

Verily, verily, I say unto you, He that believeth on me, the works that I do shall he do also; and greater works than these shall he do; because I go unto my Father. John 14:12 KJV

Whether you believe in Jesus or not, you have to admit, who-ever He was, He was causing a stir. It is really difficult to en-slave people, if they are being told they are children of a powerful Creator that has blessed them with the abilities to self preserve.

This guy had to go.

We were fortunate to have gospels written about Jesus' teach-ings. However, many of those gospels were lost, or removed. You may have heard of the gospels of Matthew, Mark, John and Luke, but what about the gospels according to Thomas, Mary and Enoch?

And, what about Jesus; who was a Jew; what did He read? It is said that He studied the Greek Septuagint version of the Old Testament. (it wasn't called 'Old' back then).

The original Bible was written in Hebrew, later translated to Greek. This Bible included the books called the Apocrypha.

After the New Testament was published in 1534, and, then re-vised in 1535; John Rogers, combined the New Testament with as much of the Old Testament as he had been able to translate in 1537. Even though he scripted it using a pen name, Thomas Matthews, he was eventually captured and put to death. (Hmm, there we go again, killing spiritual teachers.) This Bible is now called the King James Version. And, in 1884, two-hundred and seventy-four years later, the Aprocrypha was removed from the KJV. These are 14 books of the original Bible. During my re-search, I learned that aprocrypha translates from the Greek and means, "those that are hidden."

The Authorized King James Version separated these books be-

cause the Bible says in the Book of Esdras 14:46 (Ezra):
But keep the seventy last, that thou mayest deliver them only to such as be wise among the people: For in them is the spring of understanding, the fountain of wisdom, and the stream of knowledge.

They decided you weren't smart enough to have that information. We now have a Bible that has been translated, revised, edited and WHAT ELSE? You may also be interested in knowing about the Dead Sea Scrolls.

The Dead Sea Scrolls were discovered in eleven caves along the northwest shore of the Dead Sea between the years 1947 and 1956. The area is 13 miles east of Jerusalem and is 1300 feet below sea level. Some interesting facts include:

• Prophecies by Ezekiel, Jeremiah and Daniel are written in the Scrolls but not found in the Bible.

• The Scrolls appear to be the library of a Jewish sect. The library was hidden away in caves around A.D.66-70 as the Roman army advanced against the Jewish rebels.

• The Dead Sea Scrolls were most likely written by the Essenes who called themselves the Sons of Light during the period from about 200 B.C. to 68 C.E./A.D. The Essenes are mentioned by Josephus and in a few other sources, but there is no mention of them in the New Testament.

• The Essenes were led by a priest they called the "Teacher of Righteousness," who was most likely killed by the establishment priesthood in Jerusalem.

• The Essenes claimed to be "the holy ones," who resided in

"the house of holiness," because "the Holy Spirit" lived in them.

- The Dead Sea Scrolls contain the last words of Joseph, Judah, Levi, Naphtali, and Amram (the father of Moses). The scrolls contain previously unknown stories about Enoch, Abraham and Noah.

Although the Qumran community, where the scrolls were found, existed during the time of Jesus' ministry none of the Scrolls refer to Him, nor do they mention any of His followers who are in the New Testament.

It has to make you wonder, how much do we really know, and how much of it is FACT? Perhaps the miracles Jesus performed are true, but the church wanted you to believe that He was the only one who could perform such feats. Anyone else who attempted these mystical practices was doing the work of the devil and must be eliminated.

Today, more and more people are leaving the churches. We are now free to leave our congregations, but in the 12th century the Catholic Church began charging people with heresy. Heresy merely means having a belief or theory that goes against an establishment. Defying the church was a serious crime. Thousands were murdered as the church swept in and acquired their land. Some were given a lesser sentence if they confessed. They were lucky to only receive a public whipping or sent to prison.

This practice spread across Europe for hundreds of years and eventually found its way into Mexico. It wasn't until the early 19th century during the Napoleonic wars that the practice was abolished. It is astonishing to me when I realize that was only a little over 200 years ago.

But, the Americans had their share of torturing those who didn't fit in. The Salem Witch Hunts took place in Massachusetts beginning in 1693. An Indian slave from Barbados confessed to speaking with the devil. Tituba later retracted her confession claiming she was beaten and forced to confess.

Just prior to the witch hunt, the colony of Salem was experiencing a lot of struggles. There was piracy, illness and the King and Queen of England had just revoked the Massachusetts Bay Colony Charter. The residences of Salem were extremely worried and fearful of their future. Being devout strict Puritans they assumed it must be the work of the devil. When two children became ill, their sickness was blamed on Tituba who had recently spent some time with the children. The physician could find no cause of their suffering, so it was concluded that the "unusual woman" of the area must be a witch.

The hysteria lasted a year as 150 people were charged with witch craft. Twenty four were sentenced to a harsh death. Nineteen were woman, 4 were men and one as a 4 year old child. My goodness!

The settlers that came here from Europe were supposedly seeking religious freedom, yet they slaughtered the natives, forcing them to learn our language and take on Christianity.

It is obvious that those in power wanted to remain that way. They did so by denying you knowledge and by killing leaders, teachers, rebels and free thinkers.

Could this be why we have been silenced by our families? Were our ancestors petrified to talk of things that went against our spiritual leaders?

She

Ancient history is rich with female rulers and warriors. Spiritual practices included worshipping a Goddess or priestess.

In the early Christian church, there is evidence that women held positions equal to men. This was particularly true of Gnostic Christianity. In the first and second centuries, women were even bishops. The gospel of Mary Magdalene shows her as being a very influential spiritual leader, but this gospel is part of the apocrypha gospels that were removed from the Bible, so very few know about it.

But, all this changed in the fourth and fifth centuries, when women were degraded. Writers such as Saint Augustine and Saint Jerome called women weak and hysterical. It was even stated that a woman's hair should be covered because it was the work of the devil. In the hierarchy of the universe, man stood between women and God. And, of course we know it was Eve who is blamed for humanity's downfall.

How did all this begin?

I began digging into monotheism, (one God). History shows us we were once polytheistic. What happened to turn that around? Note: Much of history is speculated based on evidence that would "suggest" something. Ancient ruins, biblical scripture, artifacts, mystic teachings, etc. are just clues to our history. We have to look at these things with an open mind and do some reading between the lines.

There is some evidence showing the Egyptian king, Alkhenaten, after the 5th year of his reign, (1353-1336 B.C.) only allowed worship of one god, the sun king - Aten. But, huge temples and local communities relied on worshipping many gods and goddesses for economic reasons. The population and their priests did not approve.

Historians say Judaism was the first to abolish polytheism and proclaim there is only ONE Almighty God, but when did this occur?

According to Oxford scholar, Raphael Patai, the Book of Kings, suggested God had a wife named Asherah, but most of these texts were removed.

Excavations in Jerusalem have discovered numerous figurines and female idols of worship, including Asherah. Also archeological digs in the Sinai desert uncovered pottery with the inscription asking for blessings from Yahweh (God) and Asherah, indicated they were a pair.

These artifacts date back to the period when Jerusalem was overthrown by the Babylonians and their temples (587 BC).

It is written in 2 Kings 24:20: *For because of the anger of the LORD this happened in Jerusalem and Judah*

It is presumed that this is when the Jews became monotheistic. They believed the city and its temples were destroyed because they were worshipping other gods. In order for God to return His love and blessings, they had to ditch the other gods, including the wife. Studying the history of the Bible and the Jewish Tanakh is extremely complex. We have to remember it was translated and not every word can be translated properly. You also have to add perspective and agenda.

While one group of historians say Asherah is a female goddess who was Yahweh's wife another says Asherah means 'Sacred Tree'. In one school of thought, the name is a powerful wife of God, in another she is merely timber. Boy that was a fast chopping! You have to think of political implications as well. If there is only one God and one king who is your middleman to God, then that made the masses easier to control.

The whole idea of going to someone else for God's grace always seemed strange to me. I was raised somewhat Catholic, but far from devout. I was required to take the Sacrament of Penance. It sounds nice, but as a young girl all I can remember was going into a dark scary confessional booth to tell a priest, whose face I was forbidden to see that I had sinned. Now, talk about the innocence of children, I remember going to my mom and saying, I had nothing to confess. I didn't feel bad about anything.

She said, "Surely there must be something you did wrong?"

Really? Is lying to my brother about taking his gloves a crime worthy of all this hoopla? Besides, I believed God already knew everything and wasn't upset with me. I actually had to make stuff up that day. See, we aren't born with guilt, we are taught it. And, you don't have to buy a new dress, and go into a dark wooden box to be forgiven.

But, let's get back to the woman. According to traditional Judiasm, women were said to be endowed with a greater degree of "binah" (intuition, understanding, intelligence). I read that in the traditional text of the Tanakh, it is stated that God loved women more than He loved men, but I couldn't find any direct documentation on this. I am guessing jealousy may have played a role here.

Women give birth. That is a pretty amazing feat that man cannot perform. An ignorant man might see this as threat to their hierarchy, thinking surely God loved women more. Women also have a stronger, natural bond with their children. Once a women gives birth, her attention is put fully on her child, the man is tossed aside. I have had men confess to me that they felt some envy when the first child was born. Seems odd, but I also know women who are jealous of a man's truck or guitar. One minute you are the world, the next, not so much.

Envy is considered one of the 7 Deadly Sins according the Roman Catholic Church. We have all witnessed the acts of an overly jealous person. It's not pretty.

Traditionally, women have also been healers. Their wisdom of plants and herbs was extremely valuable. Healing people was done from the heart as their knowledge was often given for free or bartered for small gifts.

As the Middle Ages progressed, men began to get in on the practice. They charged lots of money for their surgeries, potions and blood sucking leeches. Herbal remedies were now quackery and only a male who studied at a university could practice medicine. Women were now witches that were to be burned at the stake. They were no longer healers and nurses but instead doers of black magic responsible for death, illness, poor crops, etc. If something went wrong, look for the closest female.

Ghana Witch Camps

I recently learned about witch camps that exist today in Ghana. For decades, women have been banished to segregated camps on suspicion of witchcraft. These camps contain approximately 100 women who have been out- casted by their families and communities. The woman live in small adobe huts, many with their children, while the male chief lives in what is described as a "palace".

You need the chief's permission to visit the camps and reporters claim that the chief must stay by your side while you tour the camp and interview the women. They are never left alone to speak with the females. One reporter claims when the women were asked if they were well, they all glared over at the chief and replied, "yes" as if it was required of them.

There is no reason to be frightened of these old, frail women; the chief took away their powers and as long as they remain in the camp, no one can be hurt by them. However, the women are subjected to violence if they re- enter the villages. It goes back to the need to feel safe. They can leave if a family member asks for permission from the chief, but many remain out of fear.

The idea that women with paranormal powers are evil and far less superior to men, is so evident in American culture. The first thing that comes to my mind is in 'The Wizard of Oz', when Dorothy says to Belinda, "My, I never heard of a good witch before."

And, do you think JK Rowling would have been so successful if her books were based on a character named, Harriet Potter?

Our super heroes are primarily men, even our spiritual leaders and authors. I did a quick internet search and discovered a list of the 100 most influential spiritual people living today. Nearly 80 percent were men.

When you think of highly spiritual people, you might think of monks who spend years in meditation to be enlightened, but in many regions of India only men can be yogis and study alchemy. Women are treated poorly. Their only purpose it to re-produce. They are often denied medical treatment and left in the streets to die.

So much for enlightenment!

With further contemplation, you will see the attitude of magical men and evil women played out over and over again in our books, movies and pop culture. But times are changing. Women are reclaiming their power. This is fantastic but I implore that we be nice about it. There is no need to bash the masculine. We are meant to live harmoniously. It is how we create!

THE REAL US (and we're not crazy)

Chapter 9
Reopening Our Toys in the Attic

So, what can occur when you are forced to conceal your gifts? I can tell you from my own experiences and from talking to others it can lead to depression and even self sabotage.

This is from an interview I did with Denise Ramon:

As a young child, I would see spirits. I knew they were dead, so it scared me. I also began to realize that I could prophesize. In other words, I knew things were going to happen before they actually did. This too was frightening because I had no control over it. I didn't know anybody else who could do this and I was very uncomfortable talking to anyone about it. I must be going insane, I thought. Because it became so overbearing and I had no one to support me, I learned how to shut it down.

Drinking helped cut off my connection. When you numb your body and mind, you also numb your spirit.

But, then I found myself in an even worse state. I had to stop and get my life back in order. It was then that everything turned around. My abilities grew, but in a positive way, I knew I was loved by God and no longer afraid.

Denise decided it was time to use her gift to help others. She is now a public medium and intuitive healer. Denise mends the wounds of grieving souls. The feeling of loss and even regret can be transformed when Denise connects you to your passed loved one. It gives her clients the reassurance that life continues. We never die, we just change forms. Our loved ones are no longer suffering and they certainly aren't holding any hard feelings towards us. There is no guilt or wrong doing spilling down on us from the other side, just pure unconditional love. From what I hear, life on the other side is spectacular. You can learn more about Denise at: http://www.DeniseRamon.com

The ability to "turn it off" or shut down is also common among those I spoke with. I know for myself, that when I was belittled by others, I no longer had the desire to participate in spiritual play. In the beginning, you don't know what to do when you discover there is more to you then what you have been told. No one taught you how to use these abilities, or even acknowledged they were real. You think, "Surely if all humans are capable of ethereal experiences then why aren't we all having them?"

We could be using our gifts to enhance our lives. If everyone knew they had an intrapersonal relationship with sources beyond our five senses, we could cure hunger, poverty and end wars. No one would need to be frightened or worried. We would know that we are protected, guided and loved. But, here is the kicker, WE DO KNOW, and that is why we have become a disconnected, lonely society, clinging on to any form of acceptance. Our greatest source of unconditional love is cut off and we spend our whole lives trying to find it.

The deepest holes in our hearts are yearning to merge the small sparks within us with the immense fires that surrounds us. Instead of given the key to unlock these powers, we have been shamed and bullied into keeping them hidden.

All children come to this planet, knowing they are magnificent. All souls come with an agreement to make the planet a better place. We were given the tools and the assistance. We have guides, angels, ancestors and more pulling for us. But no one wants to be the freak, so we make a solemn decision to place our memories of a mystical network into a colorless box with all of our other childhood toys. In the back of the closet, they become forgotten friends. We trade them in for a mundane existence of spiritual isolation.

Trees of wisdom

I was introduced to John Railton when he posted some of his photos on a Facebook Group. John Railton was one of those children who was enchanted with the sacred, but put away the desires to explore more, until he was an adult. I am glad he did and I am certain you will be too. Here is his story:

I have been attracted to sacred sites all my life and was lucky as a child to be taken to places such as Stonehenge and Avebury. I always felt happy at these sites and would wonder about what they were used for. My imagination would wander at these places. I have always been connected, but after my dad died in the early 90's I decided to turn it off, since I experienced some strange happenings.

In 2007, I took my first orb picture in a haunted tin mine in Cornwall UK. Whilst some people told me it was purely dust, I knew it was a special picture of the energy of a tin miner. When I was looking after my preschool children, I would go out with my mum to ancient churches. Again, I captured orbs at these sites.

Around this time I started dowsing with a pendulum and I was able to do many amazing things, such as navigation, finding people and working with energy at energetic sites. My sister introduced me to dowsing and has helped with my development. Many have helped me and without this support, I would have gone mad. I have also had to learn how to handle negativity from others regarding my work.

I have suffered with depression most of my life and one day I said looking up to the sky; I don't want to suffer like this anymore. After this, I started seeing hearts everywhere.

Also, I had many signs such as seeing robins as messengers. I helped free two that had become trapped, one in a house and one in an ancient church. It was at a dowsing club, where I was introduced to the Oldfield filter. Straight away I was capturing amazing images which many people were saying they could see spirits and light beings in.
These comments made me carry on and I started to mirror the images a year later that really started to show the hidden.

My photos became clearer and clearer. I was shown techniques in my dreams/ everything was improving and my connection was becoming stronger and stronger. I was capturing many Lyrans in my photos, as well as animal spirits, star family fairies and tree spirits. I call them light beings to keep things simple.

I have put a lot into my photography and video work and spirit has been near me when I'm out taking photos. I have been shown how to do something I call sun projection, where I stand by a tree and the camera is behind me and sunlight is used to project spirits and light code onto my back. I believe Native Americans did this on walls with fire light and the sun. After a light language channeling with Linda Hack, I was linked to being a Native American in a previous life. Also the Celtic God of nature shows up lots in my photos and I have a particular

tree I work with in an ancient Yew Forest.

It's been an amazing journey with discovery after discovery with my photos. I have plans to go to more sacred sites this year and look forward to more spiritual development. Many people on social media have supported me along with my sister. It can be a very lonely path and difficult who those around me who don't understand what I'm doing or the significance. I lost the sight in my right eye at an early age and I had seen this as a curse, however, now I have been shown that I have a gift that goes way beyond normal vision.

I'm meant to share my work and I intend to take people to the sites to connect them to the energy in the near future. This work has helped with my depression, since when I'm taking the photos I'm at one with nature and in the moment. My gift is to show others the hidden which many have forgotten. It's a connection to nature and source which in my opinion has been programmed out of us.

John Railton

You can see more of John on Facebook and YouTube:
https://www.youtube.com/user/jlwrailton
http://www.johnrailtonspiritualart.com
https://www.facebook.com/John-Railton-Spiritual-Art-450057108714518/

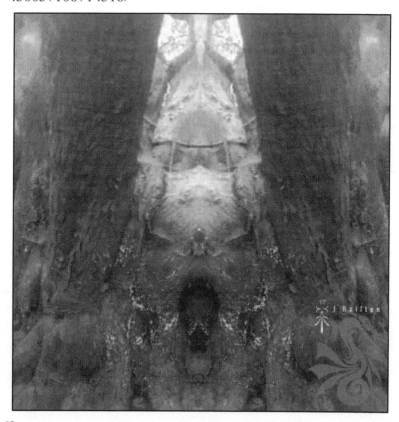

THE REAL US (and we're not crazy)

Chapter 10
Beyond the Veil

Michael Christopher is another medium, but unlike Denise and others I have spoken with, Michael was in his 40s when his gifts came to light.

The television show was entitled "Crossing Over" and it aired back in the early 2000s; the show was hosted by John Edwards who communicated with those who had passed on and was giving their loved ones messages from the other side. The first time I saw it, I found myself completely intrigued and fascinated! It led me on a quest to learn more. I began to read countless books by other mediums such as Sylvia Browne, Lisa Williams, and James Van Praagh. For reasons I can't explain, these books brought about this feeling of peace and comfort.

In June of 2010, my kidneys failed. I remember thinking that I did not want to go on, I wanted to die. In some irrational way, the thought of fighting for my life scared me more than death. But, then one or two days after finding out my kidneys failed, this feeling came over me. I had this brief thought that I must fight. I then remember literally looking up to the big man upstairs and giving "him" an ultimatum. I said, "If I am supposed to be here, for whatever reason, you need to help me find a kidney within one year. If I don't find a kidney within a year, I'm checking out because I'm not going to live on a dialysis ma-

chine." Within six months, I had a kidney donated to me!

Five years later, in the summer of 2015, my sister Jackie was murdered. It's a long story but, Jackie and I never had the chance to meet. She was born to my father's second wife. Shortly after she was born, I left for the military and through the years the opportunity to meet never happened. The sorrow and guilt of never getting the opportunity to meet her caused me much grief. Then one morning, about two months after her passing, while making breakfast, I felt a presence behind me. Suddenly, Jackie entered my consciousness. In my mind, I saw her standing right next to me. I could feel her. Then she laid her head on my shoulder and hugged me! It was so real! I just froze! This experience lasted about 20 seconds and then she was gone.

A mediumship reading later confirmed that this experience was real! Jackie did, in fact, pay me a visit! Then the bombshell hit, I was told I was a medium! At first, I did not want anything to do with being a medium, but, I would later find that not being a medium was not an option for me. Events following the visit from my sister started to present themselves one after another and my abilities came on very fast and very clear. I began to meet people that would help me along this path; some are mediums and others are teachers and I'm thankful every day for each one of them!

I now understand these events were perfectly aligned to help me develop and grow into the evidential medium I am today.
www.michaelchristopher.org

I have gotten to know Michael over the past few years and I can tell you, he has some interesting tales. I also used his talents to "bring in" a recently deceased acquaintance of mine. My son's doctor was found floating in a river and it was declared a suicide. Everyone that knew him, said, "NO WAY". Dr. Bradstreet was very popular in the autism community and there was reason to believe he was murdered. Michael knew nothing about Dr. Bradstreet or what he was involved in. When Michael made contact with Dr. Bradstreet, I asked detailed questions that Michael would never have known the answers to. He was spot on with all of it. Dr. Bradstreet was even mentioning names of other people that we both mutually knew. Not to make light of the situation, but it was refreshing to hear Dr. Bradstreet's attitude hadn't changed a bit. He was a sweet, loving man, with a spark of arrogance. Even on the other side, he is still a smart ass.

When confirmation is made without a shadow of a doubt, it really softens the grief.

THE REAL US (and we're not crazy)

Chapter 11
Flying High

Chris Johansen is one of the lucky ones. He was raised in a family that did not instill fear into him. Here is what Chris sent me:
I am a psychic medium. I am actually a 3rd generation, from what I have been told. I never studied how to do this, it just ran in my family. At the age of 8, I would astral project as I went to sleep. It was one of my most peaceful times. I would pick a place to go and off I went. Even though the gift came from my dad's side, my mom was the one who nurtured it and showed great interest in what I was doing. Unfortunately, life got in the way and doing readings for others took a back seat as I began to work full time to take care of my own family. Many years later, I decided to form a group called Casper Paranormal Research. My gift actually began to grow and it was as if I never stopped. I have worked on murder cases, was filmed for television series and I am also mentioned in many books. My abilities continue to grow and I now have a metaphysical store in Stuart, Florida. My wife's name is Genie, so we thought it would be appropriate to call it Psychic and the Genie. I am living the dream.
Chris Johansen
http://www.psychicnthegenie.com/

Chris mentions astral projecting. Astral projection is also called an Out of Body Experience or OBE. If you do any research on OBE, you will find there are many names for a variety of experiences, but let's simplify it by saying it is when your soul (your non-physical) leaves your body (physical). Sometimes it may just drift over your body — watching. This has been documented by people that were in surgery or near death. Some claim to leave their physical form and travel.

Out of body

I promised you that you would hear more on John. John is one of those guys who likes to research and study. In fact, he performed his own little experiment pertaining to OBE.

I really started seriously pursuing a spiritual journey after I had an Out of Body Experience. I was taking some psychology classes; I have always been interested in why people do the things they do. In one of the classes we were studying sleep patterns, circadian rhythms and dream. I stumbled across a forum on the internet discussing lucid dreams, astral projection and out of body experiences! It was the first time I had ever heard of those terms and I thought the people were just batty; misinterpreting the power of the mind. I decided to try to prove all those people wrong. I was going to do some experiments on myself. I was going to use the scientific method, critical thinking, and carefully document everything I did.

The first few weeks nothing happened. I just wrote down the times I would try and document that nothing happened. But, somewhere around the two-week mark, I started hearing extremely loud screeching sounds. I would have sworn there was a jet outside my house gearing for takeoff or sometimes it would sound like a truck crashed into the side of my house. I mean these sounds were so incredibly loud; it boggled my mind no one else in the house could hear them! But, I didn't let it drag me off track — I had a mission. I documented the findings and pressed on. A few days after that I started feeling these vibrations! My whole body was shaking. All my medical training pushed me towards; I was having a seizure or heart attack! So I would just check my vitals... My body was calm... My body was fine, but, it didn't feel that way. I felt like I was going to vibrate right off the damn bed! But, just like the loud noises, I didn't let it pull me off mission. I just, documented the findings and pressed on. Once I got over the initial shock of it all, I decided if all this was going to be was some loud noises and some vibrations, I was going to make them last as long as I could and that's what I did. The next time I felt the vibrations I just let it happen and I tried to see how long they would last. As I was lying there, with clearly a jet in my backyard and vibrations that could only be explained as grand mal seizures, they suddenly stopped. Like complete silence. I thought, "oh no, I must've done something wrong. I am going to have to start over!" I went to sit up and I heard this duck tape type or a Velcro type ripping sound. Really loud "RIPPP" and there I was out of my body! "Oh, my God! This can't be," I thought. I had detached and I saw myself laying there. I didn't even recognize myself. I thought what a weird looking dude! I didn't get very far, I just sort of moon walked around my room for a few minutes, but, I snapped right back into my body and I started writing all these different sensations down.

I noticed in the mirror my eyes had a pharmacological response; my eyes were dilated the size of nickels! After that I had many more OBE. I found out that I could receive a download of information during these experiences. The issue was I didn't know what the info was and I only realized it afterward when someone would ask me a question; I would just have the answer and wouldn't quite understand why or how I had the answer.

So, by trying to prove Astral Projection didn't exist I inadver-

tently proved it did and the report became a how-to list to help people have their own experiences. I might be a little biased here, but, I think astral projection is one of the few things you can do where you can really jump start your personal growth journey fairly quickly. There are a few other things I think can be sort of a cheat code on this whole spiritual journey stuff...

...But, that's another story.

After meeting John, he sparked my interest. I had heard about OBE and I had played around with remote viewing. Remote viewing is being able to see what is going on in another place. You can see the surroundings and who is there, or you can tune into another person and in your mind's eye, see exactly where they are. I notice this can happen to me without me trying, when it comes to my children. Maybe it is a mommy sense since we do share much of the same DNA.

I thought if I could do this while I was awake then doing it while I slept would be easier. The reason being is because while you are fully awake you are in a Beta brain wave state. Your brain is active and running between 12 and 40 Hz. Don't get too hung up on the frequencies right now, it is just to illustrate that this state of awareness is higher than in comparison to Alpha and Theta.

Alpha, which runs between 8 and 12 Hz, is the state you are in when you are deeply relaxed in which you are still very aware of your surroundings, but may daydream, visualize or simply slow down. You are not fully focused, but instead may be slipping into Theta, which runs between 4 and 8 Hz.

In Theta, you have intense creativity, your emotions peak and you have a stronger connection to yourself and others. This is also the state of mind where hypnosis takes place, and it is where you can tap into the subconscious. It is where psychics, mediums and shamans go while doing a "session". They may not know it is called that, but we don't need to have labels to perform an act. If walking was never given a term, you would still be able to walk and so on. I think you get it. So when a person is fully awake in Alpha state; they often have to make an effort to get into Theta. This is why you may see them close their eyes, take deep breaths, etc. It's like turning off one part of the brain and activating another. With practice this gets easier and comes faster. Soon it will be effortless. This is why Chris said he is still growing. Now that he spends more time doing sessions with clients, he has become a finely tuned and oiled machine. With practice it becomes more and more clearer what thoughts, messages or visions are your own and which ones are from beyond. They sound, look and feel different.

When you are doing something mundane such as driving on a long road, washing dishes, chopping celery, the brain waves slow down. You have done these tasks so many times you don't really need to concentrate. You are most likely in the Alpha-Theta range during these activities, and I will bet you anything, that this is when you are having your psychic moments!!!

While you are sleeping, your brainwave activity slows to 0- 4 Hz. You are now in Delta. Delta is a deep sleep. Sleep is often when we dream. And, I never met a person that did not once say, *"The dream was so real."*

It seems so real because everything is so vivid. We are fully present and aware. Our mind and eyes are clear with each detail. But all these characteristics are when our brain is in the Beta state, when we are awake. How can this be happening when our brain's waves slow down to Delta state when we are sleeping?

Are we leaving our bodies behind to rest in Delta while our soul travels in Beta, fully conscious?

If you would like to learn more I suggest, *Astral Dynamics: The Complete Book of Out-of-Body Experiences* by Robert Bruce.

But, I have to be honest, I couldn't finish it. It freaked me out. You know that fear thing?? Although I can recall experiences in my sleep that I bet were astral projections, I don't want to learn how to do it. I will let nature take its course. If I am set to fly, then I will. I would never force myself on a plane that I was not given permission to be on. Hey, they might throw me out.

Hey, Mom!

(A story submission from Joann Xydias)

I was about 8 years old, in 2nd grade and my mom was brought to the hospital. She had been bit by a brown recluse spider on her leg and they decided to keep her overnight for observation and it was extended to a few days.

I desperately needed my mom. It was October, and I was in a small school play that evening. It was a nursery rhyme themed play and I was Little Bo Peep and my mom couldn't be there to see me. My grandparents drove me to school to be in the play, and all I could think about was not having my mom there and wondered whether she missed me as much as I was missing her. They (my grandparents and my dad) wouldn't take me to see my mom at the hospital either because of their work obligations or caring for my brother and me; or, it was because it was too late in the day or they didn't want me and my brother spreading germs, I don't know.

That evening, I had an incredible and vivid dream. I dreamt my mom was just outside my 2nd story bedroom window. I could see her as clear as day and she was calling to me and telling me she was alright.

In the dream, I was trying to open the old painted shut window. I tried and tried, but I couldn't open it. My mom blew me a kiss, waved to me and said she'd see me very soon.

It wasn't until I was in my late teens when my mom told me about the brown recluse bite and how traumatized she was not being with us (my brother and me).

I told her that I knew she was going to be well as I had seen her in my dream. She said she dreamt of flying to the house and knocking on the window of my bedroom.

I interjected and asked if I had trouble opening the window and she looked at me and said that I couldn't lift the window pane. We realized after further dissection of our dreams that we shared the same type of what it known as an 'outer body experience'. We both desired to be with each other and were only able to do it via a dream state.

I asked where she went after waving bye, she mentioned she had traveled to my brother's window, but he was sound asleep and never stirred when she called to him.

Joann Xydias and her mom, Maria, are students and clients of mine. I am ever so blessed to have met them and Joann's precious son, Peter. I have to add that one day during a session with Joann, so many spirit friends of hers came to visit. The love coming through was so overwhelming, I began to cry. Until you feel this, you just have no idea how much we are loved. It is indescribable.

THE REAL US (and we're not crazy)

Chapter 12
Light Beings

Sarah and Ian were about to have a baby. Sarah had already dabbled in the world of metaphysics and was just beginning her journey into discovering that there is more than meets the eye. In fact, it was when she became pregnant that her abilities began to escalate. But, as Sarah lay in her bed having contractions, it was her husband that had a remarkable vision. While by his wife's side, a bright spark in the corner of the room caught Ian's attention. Although he was deeply focused on comforting of his wife, he could not help but to look over. The light coming from the ceiling was brilliantly colored in a multitude of hues. It was a twisting, turning rainbow that was spiraling toward them. Although one would need to blink from such a magnificent vision, Ian could not take his eyes away. He was mesmerized but only for a few seconds as the rainbow of lights shot into the womb of his beloved Sarah. Immediately, Sarah's contractions greatly increased and within minutes a daughter was born.

What I have observed in my own life and through interviewing others, is that when you have a phenomenal occurrence that is far above the norm, the experiences begin to happen more rapidly. We may all be able to tell a little psychic story like when we knew who was calling (without caller ID) or when we ran into someone we were just thinking about, but when a really big one happens, LOOK OUT! It means you have reached a higher level of consciousness and things are about to get wild.

It is again when that word crazy comes in. You ask yourself, "Is this real, and if it is so, why is this happening to me?" The anxiety builds because you don't know when it will happen again. You have no control over events. Surprises are nice when your husband brings you flowers, or a loved one shows up at your door for a visit but what about spirits showing up in your room in masses?

Sarah's delivery was a marvelous incident, but what happened afterwards was a bit daunting. Sarah informed me how it became impossible to sleep. With her beautiful new baby by her side, Sarah found herself confronted with spirits everywhere. And, although none appeared to be dangerous, it certainly was frightening. Whether an entity is solid or ethereal, no momma wants a room full of strangers.

Sarah, a beautiful mom of three with one on the way is a doula, Reiki practitioner and Integrated Energy Therapist.

It is often in these times of distress, that we need to learn how to ground ourselves or to simply shut those doors.

If you are having incidences that are unfavorable to you, please view the suggestions at the end of this chapter.

In the meantime, DO NOT BE FRIGHTENED. No harm can come to you, unless you allow it. The majority of spirits that visit are divine and benevolent, others are just lost. Sometimes they just like company, other times, they are merely being playful.

If you ever encounter one that makes you feel threatened or

nervous, your fear will encourage their visits. Lower entities hang out with lower vibrational people. What that means is, if you are fearful, depressed or experiencing any negative emotion such as jealousy or anger, you give off a vibe. It is like sensing a person's mood or disposition as soon as they walk into the room. Well, lost spirits sense it too. These lost souls are literally looking to hang out with someone. Some do not realize they are even dead and often they will seek out people who are down and out.

Did you ever notice the sign "Wine and Spirits" outside a liquor store? This is not a mistake. It is known that alcohol often calls in the lower spirits. This is very common for those who drink due to anger or depression. The alcohol can lower their walls of protection and invite other energies into their field of existence. I am not talking about possession, so fear not.

I am just saying misery likes company.

This brings me to another story of my own. As an adult, I got used to seeing ghosts. There are times I don't see any, and times when I see them often. And, there are times I can feel their presence. It is just like when you are alone one minute and can sense when someone else enters the room. Or being out in public and feeling as if someone is watching you only to look over to find out, it is true. Well the same is true for non-physical beings. If you allow yourself to open up to these beings, you can easily tell when they are around. If you pay attention, they will let you know. It could come in many forms... a feeling, a voice, a vision, a symbol or just a knowing. Most of the times, I just acknowledge them with a smile and say "hi", but I ignore the more dense ones. I respect their presence, but I am not interested in interacting with them. There are folks who actually do that sort of stuff. They clear haunted houses or help lost souls to cross over.

It's not my thing. I have absolutely no desire to take that on. I like hanging with the light beings.

But, one evening I went into the garage and there one stood. He was hanging out over by my ex husband's work bench, who had recently moved out. He was a bit grungy looking, very unkempt and withered.

The garage was Jim's (not his real name) man cave. It was set up pretty sweet for him complete with a fridge, recliner and television. It was obvious to me, however, that anybody who spent hours alone in front of the boob tube of negative news and violent shows could not possibly be happy. Jim created a perfect scenario for a gloomy soul to linger.

I didn't see him at first... I went out to the garage to grab something from the icebox. As soon as I entered the garage from the house, the fridge was right there so I didn't really need to look any further. But, like I mentioned before, I sensed that I was not alone.

I looked over to see who was visiting. The garage door was open and sometimes neighbors dropped by. I didn't feel frightened at all, so when I saw him, I wasn't startled, in fact, I was not surprised at all.

I thought, "well why not?"

He looked at me a little confused and disappointed, it was if he was saying, "Where's Jim?"

I responded with, "He is not here anymore so you can go now."

That was it. I didn't wait for an answer or have a magical,

"Poof" he's gone moment". I simply got my stick of butter and went back into the house. Needless to say, I never saw him again.

You must know that you are highly protected and that they simply must leave if you command it. I have heard people say that they can attach to you. I wouldn't use those words, I would just say, they like to hang around.

Want them to leave? Then tell them. Best defense is not let yourself get overly depressed or angry for long periods of time. We all have these emotions and it is perfectly normal. These are also the best times to ask for help from our kindred spirits. These are the times when we can be miraculously lifted or healed. Need an angel? Just call one in. They are always there to assist you, but due to your free will, you must ask.

Keeping Your Vibration High:
- Spend time in nature
- Prayer and meditation
- Laughing, comedy
- Light, uplifting or relaxing music
- Singing and dancing
- Exercise
- Massage or other hands on treatment
- Art, bright colors
- Fresh organic foods
- Detoxing or Fasting
- Natural cleaning and bath products
- Socializing, being with loved ones
- Feelings of Gratitude
- Self Love

THE REAL US (and we're not crazy)

Chapter 13
Sleep, Perchance to Dream

Dreams... we all have them. Some of us can recall them, others claim they cannot. Most often when we rise from our slumber we clearly remember the awkward images that flashed across our minds. We might laugh at how odd they were especially when Aunt Doris turns into the guy who owns the deli on the corner. Morphing and transforming is common and seamless.

We may ponder on the meaning of our dreams as many images are so pronounced that surely they must be symbolic. However, if you are like most folks, the dream state is quickly forgotten as we go about our day.

It is said we live in the present moment, but perhaps that is only during our waking hours, our Alpha and Beta states. As we slip into Theta, we begin to cross the threshold. What lies in between awake and asleep, the place where we can fantasize and be hypnotized?

Past life regression is a therapy used to recall experiences we have had in other lives. Now of course, this means you need to believe in reincarnation. Over 40 million Americans do. The numbers are of course is much higher on a global scale.

Before the 6th century, reincarnation was widely accepted in

Christianity however, there seems to be much debate about this today. Again, we can study lost and forgotten texts, but in today's New Testament, there is plenty of scripture discussing Elijah returning as John the Baptist.

Were the bishops afraid of the claim that the institution of the Church wasn't the only option to bring "eternal life" to people?

Reincarnation became more acceptable after, Dr. Brian Weiss, a traditional psychotherapist came out of his spiritual closet and wrote, *Many Lives, Many Masters.*

While under hypnosis, a client claimed of living in other places. Her stories were rich in detail and documented historic facts. He remained a skeptic until she began to tell him about his own life and the death of his son, which she had no way of knowing. This forever changed Dr. Weiss' life as he began healing his clients through the process of past life regression therapy.

But, what about those dreams that are so real, you simply cannot forget them? What about those dreams that predict the future?

Tom Zaimes has been a student, client and now friend for many years. He had a yearning to learn more and I often wondered where it stemmed from. A mortgage broker from Philadelphia, he did not fit the mold of spiritual seekers, but it is because of people like Tom that inspired me to write this book. Our outer jobs and surroundings do not define who we really are. Although it is perfectly fine to be a CEO or a janitor, many of us choose our professions, partners, homes, etc. based on what we have been told we should do.

Everyone has an inner consciousness, and a majority people wish to connect to it more deeply. We are discovering that the outside illusion of success is not fulfilling. In other words, we intuitively know there is something more.

First off, what I had noticed when I attended metaphysical classes or gatherings, a large majority of attendees were women. In fact, sometimes there wasn't a man in sight. If a man did come, he was generally dressed in torn jeans with dreadlocks. Maybe not all of them, but you get the idea. Tom on the other hand, was a clean cut, white collar dude. This manuscript was just about complete and all submissions were in when Tom called me with a story. I thought about not adding it, but because Tom had been with me on this path for many years I felt it would be my pleasure to include him. I now see, he HAD to be here, because this book is about giving others the opportunity to see themselves in these pages.

If you are a young man wearing a suit and tie who feels drawn to ancient ruins, heart pounding drum circles, plant medicine, nature walks, or mindfulness but is uncomfortable with prayer beads, yoga and crystals, it's all ok. All that stuff is not necessary. When you open your heart and let it lead you, it is then that you will discover that it is your inner light that sparks creativity and offers solutions. We are all spiritual beings, no matter what we wear, no matter what we eat and no matter where we choose to hang our tapestry. You do not have to be a chanting vegan in hemp strapped sandals to be in touch with your true self and divine source.

And, since I am on the subject of Tom, I got to mention this: Tom loves the F-word and at times, I love it too. I justify it by saying the word FUCK vibrates the 4th chakra. Om may be ancestral and sounds much nicer, but all sounds have a frequency. If you are swearing without the intention of hurting someone, then that has a different power. "F**k you!" has a denser sound and stems from anger. So if you have a vocabulary that includes profanity, don't beat yourself up. It doesn't make you unspiritual. Just be aware of how you are using it; intent means everything.

So, here is what Tom shared with me as we chatted on the phone one evening:

Tom was a member of Toast Masters. If you are not familiar with the group we can sum it up by saying it is a nation-wide support system that helps people improve their public speaking skills. Toast Masters can be found in just about any large community, and the cool thing is, they compete with each other. They have contests, districts, states and even national contests.

The next contest was to be held Monday evening. I had no intention on entering. I enjoyed the meetings, but speech writing was just too time consuming for me. I loved going to Toast Masters, but I realized I wasn't at all into the rigorous process of writing and presenting. You are taught to write, rewrite and practice, practice, practice.

I am not one to remember dreams, but this one was so vivid. It was strange because I wasn't experiencing the dream, instead I was standing outside of myself watching myself. I could see where I was and what I was wearing. I was all decked out in my dress blazer giving a speech at the Toast Masters' contest.

The speech was fantastic. Apparently everyone else thought so too, because I won! When I woke up, I immediately wrote the speech down. I know sometimes a dream's details can fade and I didn't want to forget any of the words I had just spoken.

It was a Saturday morning and the contest was Monday. That afternoon, I contacted the Toast Master President and registered for the contest. It was nothing I planned on doing or wanted to do, but now I felt compelled to do it.

That Monday night, Tom went against some pretty polished speakers, but just like his dream, he took first place. He was blown away.

I asked Tom how he did at the Division level. His answer was, '"I got robbed!"

He ended up in 4th place, so he was unable to compete any further, but I will tell you that I heard Tom's speech and he is right... ...He was robbed. It was funny, insightful and inspirational. The title-LIFE UNTAMED.

It doesn't matter if Tom ever competes again. He learned that he was a powerful presenter and due to the content of his speech, he can now live his life in a more wild fashion.

He has learned to relax and follow his inner guidance system.

When you hear the expression 'dreams can come true', we generally think of our day dreams and fantasies. But, what about our night time dreams? Since we are primarily non- physical I am guessing that aspect of ourselves does not need 8 hours of REM sleep. So as our bodies take respite in our beds and our minds put errands to rest, what does our soul do? My guess is it has a little fun!

Can I keep it, please?

Joann shares another dream:
The first and most vivid experience I personally encountered was when I was about 7 years old.

My brother and cousins were a few years younger than me and I was expected to go to school while they stayed home to play with my mom and grandmother.

The thought of going to school with its structure and missing out on the free play with my brother and two cousins was devastating as they already had been excluding me from their games.

I had skinned my knee when I was chasing my brother for taunting me about school and was in the bathroom crying, not really from the hurt knee, but because I felt so alone. While tending to my knee, I thought about how amazing it would be to get a kitten... a kitten that would be mine and it would be my best friend. I kept quiet about my desire for a kitten, my dad was traumatized as a child by a cat on the farm - it had bit his cheek and he was adamant about not wanting us to have pets because of his experience.

Later, at night, I went to bed and I had the most vivid of dreams. A beautiful woman in blue and white robes came to speak with me in the dream. She looked very kind and loving. You could feel the warmth and her face radiated with just a slight smile.

There was a cardboard box by her feet and the box began to tremor a bit. The panel at the top of the box lifted up a little before dropping close. I looked up at the lady for approval, and then to the box. I bravely pulled the top panel back and I found myself staring at a blue eyed, orange tabby kitten. Before anyone could bat an eye, I scooped him up and snuggled with him.

I awoke with this wonderful dream that I was trying hard to keep contained, but it felt so real... I told my mom about it and like most moms, she listened and said, 'That was a nice dream, honey.'

It was a Saturday, and my aunt came by with my cousins. My aunt was complaining to my mom about some place that was closed and she didn't know what to do.

I went to go outside and there on the enclosed porch was a cardboard box. It shook as the screen door shut behind me. I ran over to the box and lifted the panel... inside was a little, blue eyed, orange tabby kitten! It was meowing at me. I reached down and just hugged him.

My mom and aunt came out to the porch where I was and my aunt relayed how she came about bringing two kittens to us. I never saw the other kitten that was in the box, I didn't want to let go of the one I wanted.

My aunt had an older, junk vehicle that was in her parking lot. The neighborhood cat had kittens under the car that was parked in my aunt's business parking lot. My aunt had collected the kittens that were only a few weeks old and was going to drop them off at the animal shelter, but they weren't open on the weekend. She stopped at my mom's home to complain that they weren't open and hoped that she would drop them off to animal control on Monday.

I begged my mom to keep the kitten and kept telling her that it was just like in my dream. She reluctantly agreed, but she had to convince my dad - which she managed to do and that was miraculous!

I never saw the other kitten in the box. I don't know what color it was nor remember when my dad brought it to the animal control.

I had my lovable cat for 14 yrs. He was a wonderful playmate! I could play dolls, dress him up and I had a loving playmate for those years. He wouldn't go to anyone else. He would chase my brother around the house. He'd battle the vacuum cleaner.

I believe Joann was visited by an angel, who brought her comfort in the night. We often go to sleep with sorrow on our pillows and as we drift off to another place all our worries, fears and pains can vanish.

Comfort among the clouds

Carmen and I met at an Integrated Energy Healing Circle that I was leading in Stuart, Florida. I want to tell you a little about our meeting as I do not think it was a coincidence.

There were about 10 people in the small yoga studio. Some were seated in chairs along the wall, others sat up on mats or cushions and others were flat out on their back spread out on the floor. Bodies were everywhere. Candi McCoy, Sarah Horridge and I did our magic.

I was trying to pay attention to make sure everyone received a mini session from one of us. There were a few lucky ones who got to receive healing from all of us. Just prior to Candi wrapping it up, I could sense this woman beside me. Since the room was so small, her head was literally next to me as I sat on the floor working on a young man. It was getting hard for me to concentrate on the gentlemen as I could sense this woman calling to me. I looked over and just as I did, her eyes opened and it was confirmed that she was telepathically drawing me closer seeking my assistance. I had no choice but to go to her even though it was obvious the sessions were over. Candi had a yoga class coming in and needed to finish up our event. As people chatted and got up from their positions, I remained seated on the floor laying my hands on the lady on the mat.

She was in need. A 15-20 minute session is not enough time for me to address some serious underlying issues, but it is plenty of time for me to read the body's cues as to what may be going on. This woman was stressed and her lower torso was screaming so.

Afterwards, Carmen introduced herself. We chatted and agreed to stay in touch. Little did I know it would be a week later.

I put out a request to my email list looking for a dream story submission. I hit the send button and before I could make it to the kitchen, my phone rang... It was Carmen.

Her story is incredible. In fact, all her stories are and I strongly encouraged her to write her own book.

Carmen and I chatted on the phone for 2 hours. I am honored and thankful that she shared with me one of the most profound stories I ever heard. Typing these words gives me goose bumps. When Carmen's mom ended up in a hospital with terminal pancreatic cancer, it didn't come as a surprise. Carmen had already dreamt about it and like many of her dreams they came as warnings. She described her dreams about tornados, robberies and her own illness. Each traumatic event in her life had been preceded by a nightly vision.

Her heart was becoming heavier and heavier while she took care of her family, her clients and her mom. It was becoming too much to bear. On January 5th she lay down to sleep — exhausted.

What Carmen remembers next is being woken up by a tapping. It was steady and loud and appeared to be coming from downstairs. She had been crying and was feeling great sorrow in her chest. Tiredly, she got out of her bed to look for its origin. Although the tears were heavy on her face, she wiped them off with determination and headed for the stairs.

At first, she wasn't sure what she was seeing, but it appeared as if the walls along the stairwell had transformed into waterfalls. The stairs became wet and flooded. Water was gushing down hard making it extremely difficult to see where she was going. In all this confusion, she could still here the consistent loud tapping. Extremely concerned about all the water, she realized that it was actually her tears that were causing the flood. She was crying so much that everything had turned to a painful pool of her emotions.

The grief was so strong, but she had to continue on in order to stop that noise. As she got closer to the living area, she could see a seagull. It was pecking on the patio doors. over and over relentlessly trying to get in.

It took much adjusting for Carmen to realize what was going on. Her crying was making her weak, her chest was heavy, but she had to see what this bird wanted as it was not going away. It clearly had a message.

As Carmen got closer to the door, the bird transformed — it was no longer a seagull, but a majestic eagle. The glorious bird opened his wings with a magnificent swoop then graciously bowed his head.

Still confused as to why this glorious creature was bowing to her in sovereignty, she then began to feel a huge presence. It was overwhelming. A brilliant light surrounded her as unconditional love embraced her.

She guessed it must have been her guardian angel preparing her for her mother's passing. The tremendous sadness was now being softened by a celestial being who wore a golden belt and colossal wings. Now she could rest.

Four days later, tragedy struck. Carmen's beloved son unexpectedly passed away. There are no words to explain a mother's broken heart. As she walked the Earth numb with grief, she still had to prepare for the death of her mother. Five weeks later, she was gone too.

As Carmen told me this story over the phone, it was almost as if I could see her face. I pictured her smile from our first encounter. She wasn't sad. In fact, there was a sense of excitement in her voice. I knew there was more and it was going to be GOOD.

At a funeral, only the body is buried; what arises from the depths of the soul is unimaginable. Much like the water that spilled down the staircase in Carmen's dream there is an overflowing of immeasurable bereavement.

As we go to sleep, seeking a peek into peace, we pray to an Omnipotent Source. Carmen is once again woken by the sounds of a pecking bird. This time she finds herself on an unfamiliar road. She is determined to see her beloved eagle friend again and walks forward. As she gets closer to the sound, she sees a figure in the distance. It is slowly coming into clear vision. It is her son!

Overjoyed to see him, they embrace. She is sobbing, but he

comforts her and asks her to stop crying.

She can't. She misses him so.

"Do you want to see where I am?" he asks.

She holds him, "Of course, son, take me there."

Her son brings her to a lustrous green pasture, the sun is kissing her face and the breeze is tickling her tears.

There under a tree sits a woman reading a Bible. It is her MOM! Her heart is lifted. What an incredible gift to see her as well. She tells Carmen that everything is wonderful and she needn't worry. There is no sadness nor illness nor pain where they reside. Her son then calls over from across the field. He is now playing football with her brother.

"The visions become more and more intense. The greens glitter unlike any color I have ever seen. The blends in the sky are far more spectacular then the blues here on EARTH," she tells me. Mesmerized by her surroundings, she notices from the clouds comes a magnificent bird. Her eagle guide has returned. As he soars, the sun reflects off the fabulous colors of his wings. Everything was magnified. She never saw such splendor. The eagle landed at her feet and once again BOWED.

Carmen woke up feeling fantastic. There was so much joy in her spirit. She got to see her family and knew they were all together. Nothing could have been better.

A few days later, Carmen decided to go visit her son's grave site. It was the first time she was emotionally stable enough to go. Her heart had been lifted by their night time visit. There was still much confusion as to why he had to go so young and unexpectedly, but there was peace in knowing her mom and brother were taking good care of him.

As she pulled into the cemetery parking lot, she noticed a small crowd gathering on the grass. At first, she assumed it was a group of mourners standing over a grave site. It then dawned on her that they were near her son's site. As she approached the tombstone across the grassy hill, she could see that they were pointing and looking at something. She was curious to see and walked faster.

But, then she stopped. Her eyes grew large, her whole being melted. There on the gravesite of her departed son sat a bold and beautiful bald eagle.

Carmen Marin works in the legal field helping others. I am sure she is a blessing to those who are in need during tough legal issues. She is obviously extremely clairvoyant, but clairsentient as well.

A clairsentient (also called empathic), is very good at their job since they can truly feel people on an emotional and often physical level, they are able to give support, guidance and even solutions that are spot on.

Many highly intuitive people often work in industries where their gifts are utilized and in much demand. A GOOD doctor, nurse or health practitioner uses their intuition often and is sensitive to people's needs. Many police officers, firemen and EMTs rely on their intuition. It not only helps a person be a better caregiver, but it can also save lives, including their own.

If you asked the average cop if he or she is "psychic" most likely they would say "No". But, if you asked them if they pick up any vibes while going into a building or while hunting down their suspect, the answer would be a profound 'YES".

In many cases, a highly sensitive or intuitive person will be drawn to certain occupations, but often many will develop it while on the job. It goes back to our built in survival mechanisms.

Everyday people are *"psychic"*. Yep, I am finally using that word. I waited until the end so you could swallow it better. Intuitive sounds pretty darn cool, but throw in the word psychic and all sorts of weird imagery and negative thoughts flow.

We don't need a swami hat or crystal ball, we can leave the tea leaves in the cupboard and the deck of cards in the top drawer.

If you want to play with those things, go right ahead. They can actually help build your psychic muscle, but they aren't a necessary part of the garb. Being your beautiful, authentic self with an open heart and mind is the best tool you have.

Chapter 14
Everyday People

In this book I discussed some folks who took their gifts and used them in profound ways. Some became healers, mediums, etc.

You may feel drawn to one of these professions, but that is not the case for everyone. When I first discovered energy healing, I wanted so deeply to learn more. I went to every meeting and class I could find. This all started in the early 2000s and because I lived in Florida, my options were limited. It certainly isn't the most progressive state, but I am happy to say things are changing. I became certified in this and trained in that. What I was discovering was that I was really good at seeing into people's past.

I recall one evening at a Psychic Development group:
It was my second time attending and also my last, as the instructor had moved out of state. The room was full of two top tables and as I entered the room through the rear entrance I paused to get a good look at the space and what my seating options were. I didn't know anyone at this meeting, but because I had been to a previous one, I knew who I sat next to was going to matter — a lot.

I asked my inner GPS and I was directed to sit on the left next to Doris (not her real name). After some meditation and discussion we were instructed to sit quietly and try to tune into our partners. The trick is to just trust and see what happens. Sometimes you can get a physical sensation, or you may hear words, or even see images. These images can be very realistic or symbolic. I read my partner Doris first. What occurred in my mind was so real, much like viewing a movie. I also had twinges of a dull pain in certain areas of my body. I don't want to tell you the details because they are not pleasant at all. I was almost afraid to share them with Doris because I felt they were too personal. I didn't want to invade her privacy, so I started out slowly by telling her some details of a family gathering that I had pictured. Long story short, I was 100% accurate and was able to pick up on the fact that she was sexually abused by a family member.

I have to tell you that when something like that happens to you, it is not a wonderful moment. It can be fascinating to be able to acquire this sort of information by just closing your eyes and focusing, but the truth was at that moment, I wasn't sure I wanted this gift. It was heart wrenching to look at this woman across from me and know what she had experienced as a child. In some sense it enabled me to have compassion for a stranger, but on the other hand, I didn't want to be able to go around and see inside of people's lives.

Many years of study and training, what I learned was you never use these abilities without asking permission. Now, obviously, she was open to being read or she would not have participated in the activity. Same goes for a client as well, or they wouldn't show up in your office. However, I have had clients that have been resistant to revealing certain areas of their lives — that's okay. Emotional trauma is often expressed in the body through layers. Like an onion, we say, you have to peel some off the top first before you get to the center. Sometimes an issue is not ready to be addressed, so you move on to what is. But, anytime you get the desire to read someone without them knowing - STOP! It isn't for you to know. There may be cases when the information just arises. In other words, you are next to someone in line at a store and Aunt Millie comes through for them, or you can feel a co-workers worries, etc.; you can't do anything about that. Just accept it. Use your better judgment to decide if you want to share the information with the individual. It may not be warmly received. They may be overjoyed or they may feel violated. Use discretion and integrity. This is not a gift you should be flaunting around and using carelessly.

A few years later I became an Integrated Energy Therapist. This is a hands-on healing modality that works on releasing negative emotions from your cellular memory. This is where I began to have the most profound experiences. Not only could I pick up on people's issues from the past, but I began to have entities come visit. It first started when I began to hear names of people. I would ask my client if the name meant anything to them and sure enough, they would tell me a mouth full. Uncles, grand-mothers, old boyfriends and neighbors would show up. Some had a message, some just wanted to peek in and say HELLO. Angels and deities made appearances as well. I couldn't see them, but I could feel their presence. When I asked who they were, they told me.

The spirit world loves to communicate with us and if someone can HEAR, well they are going to talk. Sometimes it comes in bits and pieces and sometimes it comes in symbols and even smells. They will generally come through with something that will clearly indicate who they are. For example, if your grandma loved her rose bushes you may hear the word 'rose', see a rose garden or even smell roses. She wants to make sure you understand.

For any skill to develop further, one may require instruction and plenty of practice plus a strong belief that YOU CAN! I didn't know that I could tap into another person's cellular memory until I became certified in Integrated Energy Therapy. I wasn't able to quickly contact "Creator of All That Is" until I was taught an easy method in my Theta Healer training. The more I did it, the better I got.

Like Chris, some of us may be born already fine tuned and ready to play. I have heard of people who began using their talents as children; some even charging their friends and family. Why not? You can use your gifts in exchange for money, as long as you are HELPING others or you can just use your abilities to enrich your own life, like Tom, whose gift of prophecy led him to winning a speech contest.

Do not feel that because you have discovered your gift, you have to become a shaman or something. We come to this planet to evolve and expand. We have been given the ability to communicate with an unseen intelligence to assist us in this expansion. Not utilizing our blessings would be foolish. Use it how you see fit, but remember the words of 2 great men:
1. Peter in the Bible: *"As each has received a gift, use it to serve one another, as good stewards of God's varied grace:"*
2. Uncle Ben in Spiderman: *"With great power comes great responsibility"*

I trust you will serve others responsibly!

For now, just accept who you are; a physical and non-physical being who is always connected to a source field that extends far beyond the 5 senses. Play with it, trust with the open mind of a child and see where it leads you.

This is a story from Jen Holbro ok who took her own skepticism and decided to play with it:

A memorable trip

It was just after my husband Michael's aunt passed away, that I found myself traveling with his family to Ohio for the funeral. In the van was myself, Michael, his mother, his father and his sister. At the time, we were just dating and since my future in-laws lived over 3 hours away I did not know much about them personally. Michael's sister knew of my "talent", however, his other family members not so much. Nor did I think they would be accepting with one exception, his aunt on his father's side, she was a very strong intuitive. During this period of time, 2003, I was still sometimes skeptical of what I felt or "saw". I often would question myself despite the strong validations from those I might be conversing with and giving information. That is why this particular day was so moving for me. Being skeptical of my talent, I got a lesson in trusting what is provided intuitively.

Somewhere between entering Kentucky and the Ohio border, I started to get a sense of a dog presence. It just kept rolling in my mind's eye over and over. Not knowing why or the meaning, I had to speak out of this dog, it was persistent and not going away. When that happens, I know I am supposed to mention it. I felt it was strongly connected to Michael's mom and so I approached it as I always do with those whom I feel have feelings of skepticism — on egg shells, choosing my words carefully.

This is how it went:
"Did you have a dog by chance growing up maybe named Sandy?" I asked.

"Yes we did, how did you know that?"

"It was just a 'feeling' I got," I replied.

"Yes, we had a cocker spaniel." She was amazed that I knew that. Actually, my husband and sister-in-law were amazed also because they NEVER knew that their mom ever had any animals growing up. She asked again, "How did you know that?" I recall his sister chiming in saying that I was "Psychic".

I then corrected her and said that I was sensitive to things and used the word "intuitive" or "empathic", as I felt and still do to this day, it is a more socially acceptable word. With that validation and feeling accepted, images started flowing. There was a message coming through for everyone in the van.

I went on to ask, "Who is Peanut?"

My father-in-law chimes in, "That is what my brother called his wife."

I had never heard that nicknamed used. I mention this because I used to have the tendency to question myself thinking that information was "subliminally" given to me at some point, however, in this instance, I had not heard this nickname mentioned at all. Next, I sensed the word, "Bear". This would be for my sister-in-law and she chimed in and said that her Grandfather used to call her "Pooh Bear" as in Winnie the Pooh. My husband then asked if I knew what his grandfather called him. I saw a cat, but not like any other cat. I had a sense of a more strong and larger than life type cat, a white cat.

My husband validated that he used to call him "White Tiger". Again, nothing he had ever mentioned to me. Only he and his grandfather knew of that nickname.

Lastly, I got a sense of an older woman, in a floral dress or housecoat with her hair pulled up in a loose bun. My mother-in-law said, "That sounds like my mom."

My sister-in-law, being the skeptic that she was, wanted to test me and so she went on to say, "Ask my grandmother what kind of perfume she liked to wear?"

"Your grandmother said you know better; she wears powder, not perfume!"

My sister-in-law was shocked that I knew that. A test from the skeptic, and I passed. I feel this was the time that I made a be-liever out of her and it just helped validate that skeptic inside me!

For me, this was a beautiful moment. At the time of this ex-change, I had shut myself down for many years, and despite going to "school" and learning to connect, I needed this ex-change as much as they did. To be strong in my own authenticity and to speak up among those who I felt might not be open and to be warmly validated with what I was sensing, seeing, smelling and feeling. And, it didn't hurt to be a part of changing some people's views about intuition. My sister-in-law still calls me today for insights when she is in need.

Today, I am learning to accept what is shown to me and to con-vey messages as they come in, without my filter and trusting that what is being shown is what is meant to be conveyed. That even though it does not make sense to me, it is meant for the person that is sharing the experience with me. As I open myself up to be authentic and free flowing, so are more and more exciting

*new things being revealed to me. I'm excited for this chapter in
my life and eager for more to be revealed.*

**Rev J (aka Jennifer) holds a Bachelor's degree in Metaphys-
ical Healing from Delphi University, a Bachelor's of Science
in Social Work & a Master's in School & Guidance Coun-
seling for the Deaf. She is a non-denominational, ordained
minister, Reiki Master & is certified through the National
Guild of Hyponist. You can email her at:
Thirdeyeopenserenity@gmail.com**

Maybe you're not hearing the name of your grandma's dog or
seeing images of angels in the meadows (just yet), but you are
intuitive. We all are.

Surely you can recall incidences that you brushed off as coincidence. That is up to you to decide, although I don't believe in
coincidences. When frequencies line up, they act like a magnetic force looking for contact. If one person has a need and another happens to come along to satisfy that need, this is not an
accident.

Sprouting through the cracks

I met Luna while visiting my girlfriend, Nancy, at work. Luna
was her niece and was experiencing a lot of difficulty in her life.
She was 21 with little direction or clarity. Nancy offered a place
for her to stay and assistance with acquiring her driver's license
and college degree.

I had seen something in Luna from day one and each time we
bumped into each other it became more and more obvious to
me that she had some emotional dilemmas that were bogging
her down. I had mentioned it to her aunt, but nothing was ever
done about it. Luna eventually found a boyfriend and moved
out. It appeared as if she was doing much better.

But, let's just say, it didn't work out and Luna was back.

I had a chance to grab Luna one day and pull her aside. I knew a little bit about some of her experiences and I wanted to know more. She knew a little bit about me, and also wanted to know more. I did some muscle testing with Luna to give her a taste of what energy medicine can do. She was intrigued and had a ton of questions. Luna began to open up to me and what I was learning was that she was extremely intuitive. Problem was, like so many of us, we don't know who to talk to about our experiences. We don't know what to do with them. Instead of being free to explore her gifts she was continuously being told what to do by the adults that cared about her. With the desire to please and be accepted, we tend to get tossed up in a world of what we crave and what we feel we "should" do. When this happens, nothing can move forward. When we follow what others think is best for us, it looks "right" to the outsider, but our insides are aching. I invited Luna to a Reiki circle that night. She had never been to one, but was eager to explore. Drum and Reiki circles are offered twice a week at The Scented Dragon, a metaphysical store in town. Luna had actually been there to shop, but never knew about the gatherings. Her spirit had taken her into the building, but her attention never made it past the sparkly items on the store shelves.

This was an evening her soul had been calling for. This was the evening she transformed. Luna's experience was quite profound. She told me about coming face to face with Jesus during the meditation and he had some life changing advice for her. I had never seen her so happy. She was on a spiritual high. It was obvious she had just dumped a boat load of emotional baggage, as her whole being was lighter. Even after everyone left, she continued to chat with the Reiki Master for over an hour. He was so supportive in offering her guidance on exploring her divine gifts. Luna was glowing. She was finally free to dance in the delight of knowing she wasn't alone.

A few days later, Luna moved down to Ft Lauderdale to stay with her father. The last time we spoke she shared the fabulous news that her relationship with her dad was much better. Although he was still nagging her about going to college, she was happy with the job she had found. She didn't like the thought of going to school and felt she really wouldn't succeed in a class room setting. She was making enough money to get her own place and was joyfully eager to make the move. With much excitement in her voice, Luna told me about her daily practice of prayer, mediation and breath work. She had gone through a period of much needed self reflection, forgiveness and love. Finding your true self, doesn't make you a corner store psychic — it makes you a happy human BEING.

Bringing Joy

James Newman is another kindred spirit that I recently became acquainted with. I had seen James on a YouTube video and immediately knew I had to contact him for this book. The stories James offered to share here were all fantastic. I honestly didn't know which one to pick. His Facebook page, 'The Aligned Life' has quite a few good stories and he gave me permission to pick anyone. He truly is a man with great wisdom and depth. He has given me comfort in times of confusion. (Yes, we still go through periods of questioning and concerns. We're not the Buddha just yet.)

Because James' stories are available on his FB page and his YouTube channel, I decided to add a more personal one here that illustrates the power of the real us.

It is a brief encounter that surely had everlasting results:
One afternoon, while out shopping, James noticed some orchids on display. The weather had been so dreary and seeing them reminded him that spring was coming. Just the sight of them made him cheery. He decided adding one to his new residence would brighten the place up. But, instead of buying one, something told him to buy two.

On his way out to the car, delighted with his new purchase, he saw a woman sitting on a bench. James had discovered at a very young age, he was able to sum up people very quickly without ever having to speak to them. He immediately knew this woman was sad.

Without even thinking about it, James approached her and offered her one of his orchids. The woman appeared stunned. Stuck between disbelief and joy, she eagerly accepted. "My husband recently passed away," she said. "I have been missing him so much. He loved to bring me orchids."

James immediately knew why he had to buy two.

These stories are not rare. They occur when we are tuned into the real us; the "us" that is connected. When you listen to that little voice and follow its direction, things happen. I don't really like to use the word miracle because it implies that it is an unusual event, but once you begin to trust your inner guidance system, you will quickly discover there are no coincidences. Spectacular experiences are our birth right. Why would there be over 6 billion people in the world, if we were supposed to do this thing called life, alone; without assistance and interactions? I have discovered then when I do not trust my Clairs, things do not always turn out so well. I had to go through some pretty serious tribulations to finally realize my intuition was spot on after

I ignored it. If you stick logic, history and the small self into the equation, you may just miss the spiritual aspect of why something is happening, or what your next move should be.

If you worry about what others may think or feel or do or say, you are tuning out your own inner knowing. I have witnessed in my own life that when I rejected the messages and instead did what I thought was the "right" thing or the "best" thing, I kinda screwed myself in the long run. Hey, some advice is good, but make up your own mind after asking your own spirit and your divine guides what they think of the whole matter then TRUST.

Remember what I said earlier, not everyone has the same mountain to climb, so although something may be the right choice for a well intended friend or family member, it may not be the wisest move for you. Just take Luna for example, attending college is great for lots of people, but she felt it would be a complete waste of time and money. Her desire to please her dad was important to her, but when she rejected the idea, she found her bliss. You can be extremely successful without a degree and much happier if you follow your heart and inner calling instead.

It's not easy to trust yourself. That little boy in the sandbox who was told his castle wasn't as good as Johnny's is still talking to you. The little girl who wore old hand me downs and wasn't told she was beautiful is still feeling unworthy. Laughter still echoes in your psyche from when you told your older brother about your "imaginary" friends.

Remember, all we ever wanted was to fit in and be accepted. This isn't an opportunity to play the blame game or victim. That will certainly lower your frequency plus it really isn't anyone else's fault. Remember, they too come from a lineage of fear and worry; not being taught to trust. I find much of the older generation lives in a state of constant guilt. If you feel you did something wrong or bad and are being frowned down upon by a MIGHTY GOD that is angry, how could you possibly not be scared? The concept that I am going to burn in hell for eternity would certainly put me in a state of panic.

Instead, take this as an opportunity to have compassion for others, who may have unintentionally hurt your spirit. And, best of all, it is a chance to have compassion for yourself. There is nothing wrong with you.

Trust and faith may not come easy for you. This process takes time. But, when a "coincidence" occurs or your intuition is accurate, acknowledge it as a demonstration of the Alpha and Omega. Offer gratitude and know you are truly loved and blessed. It may sound silly, but when I do this, I can sense the ethereal entities smiling and I can feel their encouragement. It is almost as if they are saying, "Nice job" with a feeling of pride. The more you do this, the more you will experience the 'WOW' factor.

Be patient. Do not assume every little "sign" is permission for you to act. If you are feeling doubt then ask for clarity and wait patiently for an answer. But, stay alert; an answer may come in the strangest forms.

Patience is also a tough issue. We all want answers NOW! Honestly, sometimes I get insight or answers within minutes, other times it is just a ball of confusion. This is when I know I am not in alignment and I have some other "crap" going on. Most likely, something is lurking in my energy field or my thoughts that I have to address. When I am feeling off, sometimes I will have a dream about a past issue that I later realized must have been "stuck". A good example would be when I told myself I had for-given someone. I began to lift them in my thoughts and prayers.

When I found anger creeping back up within me, I repeated the process. Then I had a dream, I was choking the S#@T out of him. Hysterical as it may sound, a dream can be a soul cleansing when an emotion is brought to the forefront and released.

Think of it like this, before you fully clean that Thanksgiving turkey pan, you let it sit overnight in soapy water. The grime has to come lose and float to the surface for an immaculate washing.

You can convince your good, little boy and girl ego that you let it go, but truth is, your vessel is deep and you may have some layers to burn through. The healing process can be arduous.

When you are feeling rested and renewed, you are vibrating at a higher frequency. These are the times when you do get the WHAM BAM message. They come in loud and clear and with-out question, you should listen.

Detour

I had just picked my son up from his dad's house and was plan-ning on stopping at the grocery store on the way home. Anyone with a young son knows you better have that fridge stocked. I kept hearing "go home first" I thought about it and really had no reason to stop by my place first. For 20 minutes, it kept re-peating itself, "Go home first." It got to the point where I de-cided I would go home to use the rest room first. Although I didn't have the need to use the toilet, I couldn't come up with any rational reason to go stop by the apartment before I went to the store.

I pulled into the apartment parking lot happy to find a spot close to the entrance. I wanted to be fast so I could get back to my original plan. As I got out of the car, I saw a woman about 20 feet ahead of me, walking towards my building. It appeared to be Mary, the woman down the hall for me. I could see she was all dressed up which was odd for the middle of the day. She generally wore clothes that were sporty and comfortable. Today, she had on heels and a jacket. I said "hello" and complimented her on how great she looked. She turned around to see who I was and that was when I caught a quick glimpse of her face.

I instantly knew something was wrong and I instantly knew what it was. It was if information was downloaded into my brain at the speed of light. This is called claircognizant, when you just know something without any rationale. "She just got back from court for her son," was jolted into my consciousness.

I never spoke to Mary about her son and I had no idea he was in any kind of trouble. I had met him a few times in the elevator and he seemed like a nice kid so this wasn't an intelligent guess. Mary stopped in the parking lot and waited for me to catch up. I asked her if she was ok. She broke down, right there.

It was then clear to me, my sources sent me back home to console this shattered woman. Together embraced in friendship, we walked inside. Down the hall in the lobby is a small comfortable sitting area; for over an hour we hugged, we prayed and we shared our sorrows.

The Alpha and Omega knows all. It knows what we need; it knows where we are needed. There isn't a single soul on this planet that doesn't need support.

This support comes in many forms: physical and non physical.

It is said that when we lift others, we ourselves Rise. Rising is good!

When our emotions are high our frequencies are raised. Higher frequencies brings us closer to our true selves, our divine being, the real us.

Channeled guides often speak of higher vibrations, frequencies and octaves. They even claim that they too rise when they assist others.

Now, I don't know how that works, being a spiritual guide must be pretty cool in itself, but my current theory is when humans (spirits in dense form) begin to realize they are all from the same source, with individual itineraries to the same destination, compassion will spread, and hearts will open. Since the heart is actually where the Kingdom resides, we will then have Heaven on Earth. It is a win-win for everyone, even them!

This is why what we once called 'paranormal' is now becoming the new normal. Assistance is making itself known. Your gifts are needed. No matter what your abilities are now, they will increase with great care, respect and responsibility. When you come out of your spiritual closet and begin engaging in conversations with others, you will clearly see that this is not just a weird, "crazy" thing that is happening to you. It is happening globally and at a much faster pace.

We are here to rise above the limiting beliefs that we are small and insignificant.
The Real Us...
Is Powerful, Magnificent and Unconditionally Loved..
Don't forget it.

Stay in touch via my Facebook Pages:
- The Real Us

- Heartlinked Integrated Energy Therapy
  www.Heartlinked.org
        - Sessions and classes
        - Developing Your Abilities
        - Training and workshops

Look for *The Pocket Guide to The Real Us* with tips, and tricks to elevate your Vibe!

NOTE: The next book in The Real Us series is about our natural ability to heal.

If you would like to submit a story pertaining to recovery using natural health remedies or therapies please contact me at:
TheRealUsSeries@gmail.com

In the meantime, you may want to learn more about the science of CBD and its miraculous benefits:
        www.heartlinked.myctfocbd.com

Suggested Reading:

I Am The Word, by Paul Selig

The Science of Mind, by Ernest Holmes

Hands of Light, by Barbara Ann Brennan

Story of Edgar Cayce: There Is A River, by
Thomas Sugrue

Autobiography of a Yogi, by Paramahansa Yogananda

The Spontaneous Healing of Belief, by Gregg Braden

A Course in Miracles

Made in the USA
Middletown, DE
22 January 2019